Good News for Bruised Reeds

WALKING WITH SAME-SEX ATTRACTED FRIENDS

"Verse 11 of 1 Corinthians 6:9–11 speaks of the tremendous power and grace from God for transformation. God's Word states that people who were once bound up in all kinds of sin and brokenness—including the pursuit of same-sex desires—can be cleansed and made right with God. This book reinforces the truth and reality of this experience for anyone affected by same-sex attraction who longs for healing and wholeness. Grab copies of it and help proclaim the ongoing miracle of lives set free."

Derek Hong
Senior Pastor
Good Gifts City Church/City Missions Church

"With so much demonization of Christians in social and news media as haters of those with same-sex attraction, it is refreshing to read of Christians who reach out to them in love. May this book encourage more to do likewise, fulfilling the command of our Lord to love our neighbours as ourselves."

Bishop Terry Kee
The Lutheran Church in Singapore

"There is a real need for greater understanding and openness within our churches about issues of sexuality. This collection of personal stories will certainly be a real encouragement to Christians who experience same-sex attraction to persevere in discipleship and also to help in equipping their friends and pastors to support them."

Rev Vaughan Roberts
Rector of St Ebbe's Church, Oxford
Chairman of the Proclamation Trust

"The churches in Singapore, like so many of their counterparts throughout the world, are in the midst of grappling seriously with the question of how best to love and minister to those who experience same-sex attraction or who identify as LGBTQ. Reading this book—which is filled with honest, moving, and often very difficult and challenging testimonies—will give both same-sex attracted Singaporeans themselves as well as their friends and pastors a poignant and instructive glimpse into what it looks like to be on the front lines of engaging those questions. May there be many more such books in the years ahead!"

Wesley Hill
Associate Professor of New Testament, Trinity School for Ministry, Ambridge, Pennsylvania
Author of Washed and Waiting: Reflections on Christian Faithfulness and Homosexuality

"This book contains not just stories of individuals with same-sex attraction, but also stories of those who have come alongside their friend or child on this similar yet different journey—similar because we are all fallen, broken, and bruised reeds in need of our Saviour's love; different because the journey toward sexual wholeness and personal holiness holds unique challenges for the person who experiences same-sex attraction. Most importantly, pastors speak up in this book, proving that the Church **can** be a safe place of authentic relationships, with vulnerable intimacy and transparent accountability. Thank you to the Courageous Ones who have spoken, setting the example and providing the encouragement for every one of us to make a difference, bringing shame and sin into the loving Light."

Joanna Koh-Hoe
CEO, Focus on the Family, Singapore

"Scripture tells us that Jesus who is the 'Word made flesh' came and lived amongst us as one who was 'full of grace and truth' (John 1:14). He extended a gracious welcome to all who were 'weary and heavy laden' while at the same time maintaining a firm hold of the truth of God in word and deed. The stories you will read in this book likewise reflect grace and truth, in how God's people have extended grace to 'bruised reeds' while holding fast to the truth of God's word. May we in the church learn to do likewise as we minister to the sexually broken in our midst."

Rev Jonathan Wong
Diocese of Singapore
Convenor of Lay Leadership Training

"Real words from real people. That is what this book gives us—real words arising from real stories and real struggles of real individuals. My heart has been moved by these stories, and it is my prayer that the following hope will be fulfilled in increasing measure:

'If you, the reader, are going through what I have struggled with, I would like you to know that, really, you aren't alone and God is still walking with you, even when it seems like the church is unable to... But I pray that the church will learn to walk with us, even when it is awkward and difficult, because that's why Jesus came.'

May this book help God's people bring God's good news and love to all who feel ignored or dismissed like 'bruised reeds'."

Rev Dr Gordon Wong
President
Trinity Annual Conference of the Methodist Church in Singapore

Good News for Bruised Reeds

WALKING WITH SAME-SEX ATTRACTED FRIENDS

Edited by
Joanna Hor, Ng Zhi-Wen, Bernice Tan, Tan Soo-Inn,
Ronald JJ Wong, Raphael Zhang

GRACEW⬚RKS

Walking with Same-sex Attracted Friends

Published by Graceworks Private Limited
22 Sin Ming Lane
#04-76 Midview City
Singapore 573969
Tel: 67523403
Email: enquiries@graceworks.com.sg
Website: www.graceworks.com.sg

ISBN: 978-981-11-6660-0

Printed in Singapore

1 2 3 4 5 6 7 8 9 10 • 25 24 23 22 21 20 19 18

CONTENTS

* These names and others in the individual stories have been changed to maintain confidentiality.

FOREWORD

All our thoughts and actions are ultimately referenced to God who created us and rules over us with His sovereign grace and compassionate love. This God, as revealed in the Bible and in Jesus Christ, is understood as both holy and compassionate, righteous and loving (Ps 116:5). The apostle Paul refers both to the kindness and sternness of God (Rom 11:22). These characteristics of God are two sides of the same coin. We risk losing a proper understanding of God and His ways when we lean on one side at the expense of the other.

The church, which is called to proclaim God's truth and demonstrate His love, is therefore given a role that includes having a prophetic voice as well as a priestly ministry. It is possible to focus on just one of these aspects and risk losing the depth and power of the gospel of Jesus Christ, who refused to throw stones at a woman caught in sin, telling her instead "neither do I condemn you … Go now and leave your life of sin" (John 8:11). He promised that "whoever comes to me I will never drive away" (John 6:37). The prophetic voice of the church should turn people away from sin (in whatever form) that corrodes and destroys the soul, and the priestly healing hands of the church should be extended to those who turn to Christ with faith.

These principles apply to all sinners and all kinds of sin, and the Bible reminds us that we are all sinners in need of God's redemption, healing and transforming power. This is particularly true for those who are troubled by what Christians of a different era termed as "besetting sins"— those that are deeply lodged and seem to take time to be dislodged. The Bible points to the "sin which clings so closely" (Heb 12:1, ESV). God often does a deep work of redemption and deliverance in such cases, though there are some who may experience sudden freedom from a besetting sin. For most people, freedom comes through persistent faith, spiritual disciplines, and the encouragement of a loving Christian community as the Holy Spirit does His work within and among God's people. God intends to save us not only from the penalty of sin but also from its lingering power.

In one sense, our problem is with distorted desires. The apostle Paul described people living in the terrible times of the last days as those who suffer from misplaced love: the love of money, of pleasure and, at the heart of it, self-centred love (2 Tim 3:1–5). The gospel of Christ addresses this and transforms us to become people who learn to love God wholeheartedly and who love their neighbours with true self-giving love (Matt 22:37–40).

These principles are also true in the case of those who struggle with same-sex attraction (SSA). The church is often clear about where to stand—declaring the biblical teaching that homosexual practice is sinful and incompatible with Christian discipleship. But it is also true that the church is often not so ready, or does not know how to offer pastoral care to those who turn to it for help and hope. This may create a sense of rejection among those who are seeking to find God's grace in Christ and a way of overcoming their besetting sin.

This book seeks to both encourage those who are serious about following Christ but who are struggling with SSA, and to challenge the church to lend a listening ear and a helping and welcoming hand. The stories in this book are told with pathos, honesty and courage. They introduce us to the world of those who struggle deeply with SSA, with powerful and disturbing feelings of loneliness, shame, failure, confusion, rejection, anger and frustration. They reveal the struggles of loved ones when they discover a family member who has SSA. These stories create necessary empathy and sensitivity.

This book also brings a sense of hope. The stories shared by those who minister to people with SSA reveal the compassionate understanding that is required to help people with SSA who turn to the Lord for healing and transformation. Some of the closing chapters are filled with Christian hope and an outstanding vision of a truly Christian community where all sinners can find God's truth and transforming grace. Churches are challenged not to be like the elder brother who refused to join his father in welcoming his repentant prodigal brother who had returned home, and to be reconciled with him (Luke 15:28–32).

There are various metaphors for the church; one is that it is like a spiritual hospital where we find healing and hope in the context of a redemptive community. This is emphasised in this book. Pastoral ministry has long been understood as a ministry that involves healing, sustenance, guidance and reconciliation. This should be made available to all, including those who struggle with SSA.

There are issues introduced here that would require greater exploration, such as cultural influences, the rubrics of spiritual formation, the nature of holiness, and the theology of being church. But this book succeeds in making people think more deeply about SSA and how we should respond to it, both from the point of view of those who wrestle with it, and those who seek to help. It provides encouragement to those who seek to follow Christ but suffer from besetting sins, and also brings a challenge to churches to learn how to minister to them.

In the end, we must all recognize that whatever our story or struggle with sin (and we all have struggles), God has chosen us to be His children so that we can be conformed to the likeness of His Son (Rom 8:29). This is God's plan for all, and we are all in this journey to becoming Christlike. God has not finished with us yet, and continues to work in us and among us as we keep our eyes fixed on Jesus and allow the Holy Spirit to do His sanctifying work in us. The church should understand this and provide a safe redemptive space to all of us sinners (cf. Isa 4:5–6), whatever our problem, surrounded by the sheltering canopy of God's unchanging truth and abiding love.

Bishop Emeritus Dr Robert Solomon
The Methodist Church in Singapore

GOD OF BRUISED REEDS

– Theological Overview –

Jesus was at the height of His earthly ministry: He was popular, having healed many people; He attracted broad-based support, not just unschooled fishermen, but also Matthew the tax collector and a couple of Zealots. He had multiplied himself by sending out twelve disciples with authority in the name of the Father to drive out unclean spirits and heal every disease. But He was not conventional, because He broke the culturally accepted Sabbath laws by healing a man with a withered hand, who could have been healed on another day since this was not a life-and-death matter (Matt 12:9–14). Not surprisingly, this raised the jealousy and ire of the established religious leaders who began to plot how they might kill Him.

At this juncture, Matthew 12 quotes Isaiah 42 to show that Jesus fulfils what was spoken through the prophet Isaiah about God's servant:

> *Here is my servant whom I have chosen, the one I love, in whom I delight;*
> *I will put my Spirit on him, and he will proclaim justice to the nations.*
> *He will not quarrel or cry out; no one will hear his voice in the streets.*
> *A bruised reed he will not break, and a smouldering wick he will not snuff out,*
> *till he leads justice to victory.*
> *In his name the nations will put their hope.*

Matthew the author tells us that Jesus *is* the promised Suffering Servant. The power that Jesus had demonstrated so far, in teaching with authority (Matt 5:29), healing many diseases (Matt 8:16–17) and calming the storm (Matt 8:23–27) is a reflection of God's kingdom breaking into the sinful world, and bringing about justice so that in his name the nations will put their hope. While all these are encouraging miracles of God, interestingly, that justice would also come about through a series of actions that this Servant would *not* do. Reading Isaiah 42:1–9 in this context then, Matthew is making a statement about Jesus' character, based upon all that he has done so far.[1] This character is also set in the context of the ultimate goal of his work, which is justice for all nations. We shall draw three lessons from these passages about God's character. These characteristics may be seemingly contradictory, but are held in marvellous tension in this passage, and embodied in Jesus Christ.

God's Chosen Instrument Is a Lowly Servant

In the world today, it seems that the powerful people are the ones who can make a difference. Those in government are the ones who rule the country and determine policies. There are "influencers" on social media who have many followers and who can change and influence social trends. In contrast, the one whom God chose was a servant, a lowly person. Jesus was an itinerant rabbi who came from an unfashionable town, whose parents were nobodies.

---

1   While there are minor textual differences between Matthew 12:15–21 and Isaiah 42:1–9, they are not significant for our purposes here. One commentator, R.T. France suggests that Matthew was using an "independent translation" from the Hebrew. Matthew, TNTC, (Nottingham, England; Downers Grove, IL: IVP, 1985, 2008), 210.

Even His first disciples were initially a little scathing about his origins (John 1:45–46).

These days we tend to use the word "helper" to refer to domestic workers who live in our homes and who help with domestic chores and/or caring for the young or the elderly. We prefer this term to "servant". The helper or servant is thus one who is lowly and "helps" our families. Yet, in Scripture, God calls himself our helper. For example, Moses worships God before his death in Deuteronomy 33:29, "Blessed are you, Israel! Who is like you, a people saved by the Lord? He is your shield and helper and your glorious sword." The Psalmist prays to God who sees the trouble of the afflicted because he is the "helper of the fatherless" (Ps 10:14). One reason the Psalmist can give thanks to the Lord who is good and whose love endures forever (Ps 118:1), is because "The Lord is with me; he is my helper, I look in triumph on my enemies" (v. 7). The Almighty God who created the world is willing to take upon Himself a "lowly" title or position; indeed Jesus took on the form of a servant, and bent before His disciples to wash their feet (John 13:1–17).

In the Kingdom of God, then, it is not those who are powerful, or have positions and titles, who can make a difference. Rather it is the nobodies, servants whom people often do not even see and just take for granted, who in God's strength and power can make an impact for God. Therefore in God's kingdom, there is no shame in being a servant because God himself is a servant.

God Will Not Break Bruised Reeds and Will Bring Forth Justice

God the helper is especially gentle with those who are

weak and vulnerable. He will not break bruised reeds (they are already so close to being completely broken) nor snuff out the smouldering wick (they are already in danger of going out altogether). There are many people in our communities who are wounded, either due to sin, having made poor choices, because of external circumstances or even the "sins of their fathers". Jesus healed the sick, the demon possessed, and the sick woman who had been bleeding for 12 years. By healing them, He not only gave wholeness and life, but also opened the door for them to be part of the community again.

Often healing comes from God bringing wholeness into our lives, to correct a deficit or a lack: when we have a broken bone, healing comes when the bones are made whole and fused together again. We overlook the fact that healing can sometimes be the result of choosing not to do something—we choose not to scold our child when she has done something wrong, because we can see that she has obviously learned her lesson and is repentant and remorseful already. The saying "don't hit a man when he's down" comes to mind.

Just based on this, one gets the impression that God is all gentleness and niceness. But the following verses give us a more complete picture—"In faithfulness he will bring forth justice; he will not falter or be discouraged till he establishes justice on earth" (Isa 42:3–4). Sometimes when humans chose not to extract our just desserts it seems that we are being weak or too soft. It is sometimes difficult for us to judge when to not do something. But God who knows the human heart knows when not to break the bruised reed, and yet through that, can bring about justice.

But God is gentle in bringing about justice on the earth. This is our God, and we must keep this tension about God. He is a holy God and has demands and standards. Thus, before Him we cannot make excuses about our circumstances or sin, because God's holiness demands that there be repentance. Indeed He himself has already made the way, through the cross, for us to have a relationship with him. This is no cheap grace, hence our human response must be to love Him and obey His commands.

Different values challenge us today—pragmatism, convenience, or the pursuit of self-fulfilment. For those who follow after God, it must be Kingdom standards which determine our actions. For example, this means that the sexual act is only to to be expressed in a heterosexual marriage relationship; celibacy is required of everyone else. These standards are not only hard to keep in these days of sexual licence and openness, they are also sometimes mocked by others as being backward or old-fashioned. Regardless, for those who follow the Suffering Servant, these are the values we hold on to.

God Makes a Covenant with His People So That They Can Be Witnesses to the World

God's plan for salvation is to form a people who are his covenant people and who will follow his ways. Jesus sent out his twelve disciples and gave them the authority to do what he did so as to expand his Kingdom on earth (Matt 10). When we have chosen to follow him, we do not then just sit around and feel good about ourselves. The Servant of the Lord in Isaiah is called by God to be a light for the Gentiles, to open the eyes that are blind, free captives from prison and release those in the dungeon and those who sit in darkness (Isa 42:6–7). This is the passage that

Jesus used about Himself when He preached in the synagogue in Nazareth (Luke 4:16–21).

Following the example of Jesus—as a servant who would not break bruised reeds—so God's redeemed people are to be a light to those who still do not know him, opening their eyes and freeing them from captivity. God's call to the servant can be ours today, "I will take hold of your hand, I will keep you and make you to be a covenant for the people" (Isa 42:6). When God holds us, we go in His ways and His strength. There are those who witness aggressively, and their manner turns people away from the grace and freedom of the good news. God's people are to be His witnesses in the world today, not just bringing His message, but also using His methods and in His manner.

Conclusion

Over the years, I have walked with people through the crises that they face: broken relationships, abuse and illness. In times of my own struggles I have sought counsel and help from others. I have learned much about the frailties and foibles of human nature; and also about the real presence, grace and goodness of God, mediated through people who walk with us through these situations. And thus we have the ability and grace not just to live through crisis, but also to continue to grow and flourish as human beings. All this can be so because Yahweh is a God who will not break bruised reeds.

Dr Kwa Kiem Kiok
Registrar
Lecturer, Inter-Cultural Studies
East Asia School of Theology

INTRODUCTION

What would the good news of God's Kingdom look like in a community of Jesus' people? What would such a gospel community be like for people with same-sex attraction (SSA)? How might churches be safe spaces for them to know Jesus and to grow to be more like Him? For the benefit of the Church, these questions have been brought to life by the true personal stories in this book, at great expense of, and with great courage from, their contributors.

Many churches and Christians feel ill-equipped to help Christians with SSA live flourishing lives. Conversely, Christians with SSA feel that churches could be better communities to them. We hope this book plugs the gap between Biblical teaching on sexual ethics and the gospel on the one hand, and their application to churches and Christians as gospel communities to people with SSA on the other.

The Church must embody the gospel with love, justice, and compassion. That is its calling. The Church's witness to a watching world and its discipleship of an enquiring younger generation will be impacted by how she fulfils this calling.

The stories in this book will cover a broad range of experiences. We do not advocate any particular expression as the only or best solution, but we hope that you—as a Christian and someone who can influence your church—

will better understand Christians with SSA, undertake critical self-examination and help your church become more of a gospel community to those grappling with SSA.

God-willing, this book may also be the start of a series of books which aim at answering the first question above, to spur the Church to be more of a gospel community to people who are bruised and at the margins. May we keep returning to the Good News that we are all bruised reeds, restored and made whole by Jesus, that we may in turn bring the people around us to restoration in the grace of God.

Jesus help us. To God be the glory.

Ng Zhi-Wen & Ronald JJ Wong
Editors

SECTION 1 — PERSONAL SSA STORIES

LOVE CONQUERS ALL

Somehow, Cecilia got the permission to use the air-conditioned library room. I settled down in a chair and, as usual, watched as she did her homework. There wasn't much I could help with, although I guess in this case, it wasn't so much about what I could teach her, but about being a friend, a confidant, and perhaps a role model.

> "Eh Karen, I got a boyfriend," she said out of the blue.
> "Oh. Uh, okay."
> What else was I to say? What did I care? She went on with her work.

As she continued with her Math worksheet in silence, though, a strong urge to tell her about my first relationship crept up on me. I tried to shake it off. Fought the urge in my heart. Why would I do that? There was no reason to. It wasn't relevant. She was going to think I was lonely and in need of attention, telling anyone who would listen about my scars. Or, worse still, might she think I was trying to say that I was interested in her? Might she become wary of me? Was it worth putting the friendship at stake, all because of a silly impulse?

But if this was from God and I decided not to do it, I would miss out on the opportunity to be a blessing.

What strange ways God works through. What did God

want from me, and did it require me to put my heart out there like a fool? Did God come in these ways: strange, vulnerable, foolish?

I quelled the battle in my gut.

"Um," I blurted out, breaking the silence, "I was in a lesbian relationship in secondary school, but that was a long time ago."

She met my gaze. I noticed a flash of curious realization in her eyes, still shrouded in caution, like a puppy realizing that it just might be safe after all.

"Really? ...I have something to tell you... the boy-friend I was telling you about, it isn't a boy. She's a girl."

A peep of Christ's wisdom unveiled itself to me.

Cecilia went on to reveal that she had been feeling terribly guilty about it, and that she felt unworthy to be in the presence of God. (Oh, but darling, we all are.) The previous two Sundays, she would go to church, but sit outside the hall until the service was over. At that moment, my heart felt like a flask that had been shattered to release its aroma. I knew why the Lord had grown this particular revelation in me, the purpose of the fruit of my own travail, why the Lord had brought me to her. These are the lengths Jesus would go to to tell somebody He loves her.

"You know, I do a lot of things that make my father angry. I keep coming back late. I don't spend much time at home. I'm not a great daughter. But what would be worse than these things is if I were to stop talking to him altogether. Nothing beats the relationship. No matter what you do, it isn't as heart-breaking to God as cutting off the relationship with Him."

Tears welled up in her eyes, and I could feel Jesus's love for her. He brought me into her life by a stroke of chance, all so I could tell her that He loved her when she couldn't hear it herself.

--

I was in a lesbian relationship when I came to Christ. I was invited to a youth service, and as I watched everyone lift their hands high in worship, I realized that they actually knew God. I realized that I had been living a lie; that although I called myself a Christian, I didn't actually know Him at all. I never prayed in earnest, never read the Bible, and scarcely even thought of Him as a real being. That night I gave myself to Christ in tears, wanting nothing more than to know Him. The season that followed was peppered with joyful fasting, where I spent my recess breaks reading the Word. No one at church spoke to me about my relationship. They must have known, since my girlfriend and I attended church and hung out with the cell group together. Years later, I found out that my cell group leader had told the other youths, "If you're wondering about Karen, just give her time." Because of that, I was given the space to experience the love of God unhindered. I pursued Him with joy. And as

> I didn't know what lay ahead, but I knew that the Word was slowly shaping my life with its beauty.

I pursued God, the desire for sin began to fall away. As I read His Word, revelation poured into me. Love was always gentle, and Love's edifying Word wrapped around my sins with a weighty beauty. It wasn't "Don't do this, this is wrong" that convicted me. It was "Don't you know that you are a temple of the Holy Spirit, who lives in you?" I didn't know what lay ahead, but I knew that the Word was slowly shaping my life with its beauty. Transformation is not about debating what you can and cannot do. Transformation is "not I, but He". Under the weight of His beauty, though, the problem spots naturally surfaced like red blisters screaming for the soothing balm of repentance.

One day, in the midst of yet another argument with my girlfriend, I called my cell group leader in tears. He finally said, "I think you know what you need to do". By then, there was barely any positive feeling in the relationship to hold on to. I blamed God for a while after we broke up, of course, because it's always convenient to put your blame on one who cannot fight back. But neither He nor my church had done anything more than to present me with a Love that was so much greater.

A non-Christian told me some time back that he couldn't comprehend why a Christian would refuse to date him, even though she had made it clear that she had feelings for him. "Amor vincit omnia," he had declared, an accusation. Love conquers all. Yes, it is true; Love conquers all. Under the light of the Greatest Love, all other loves stand or fall. As for me, my life and my body are Christ's; He has given Himself for me, and I give myself to Him.

- -

It has been ten years since Christ first dropped His love into me. Recently, I've been diving deeper into the Theology of the Body, of teachings about sexuality, and about the role that gender and marriage play in shedding light on the marriage between Christ and the Church. One December, as I prayed about the upcoming college semester, God told me that I was not to think about boys. "Focus on loving Me as a husband."

As a husband? I was perplexed. A silly thought cropped up: If I loved God that much, where would I have the space for my earthly husband?

And then it hit me that that was the devotion God demanded: the singlemindedness of a spouse. I was to love Him with the exclusive devotion that I would give my future husband. Like a doe, I was to be focused completely on Him, looking neither to the right nor to the left.

But oh, God. How is that possible?

There in my room, I had a vision of a wedding. In the vision, I am wearing a white dress, a white veil. There are white flowers in my hair, and the same white flowers line the aisles. Jesus the Bridegroom stands before the altar, his eyes fixed on me, smiling. Slowly, I take one step down the aisle, and then another. And every step I take down the aisle is a step of sanctification, until at last, my life is done and I am right in front with Jesus. Jesus lifts my veil, and I see him face-to-face.

Karen Ho

GOD *IS* WITH US

When did it all begin? For as long as I can remember, I've never liked wearing typically feminine clothes. Since I was a child, running around in skirts just made me feel vulnerable and not me. It could have been a phase, but my mother did not embrace it and felt there was something wrong with me. I don't blame her, because she, too, struggled with her own sense of self-worth and identity. I also grew up feeling that women were inferior to men, and that it was therefore better to be a man than a woman in this world. Being rather introverted, I kept all these thoughts to myself. It took more than 20 years before I learnt how to articulate these thoughts to people.

My parents are not Christians but I grew up knowing about God. They sent me to a Presbyterian kindergarten and a mission school, and somehow that became the basis for coming to believe in Jesus and becoming a Christian when I turned 16. However, this was not without much struggle.

I realized I was attracted to women when I had feelings for my schoolmates from the age of 13. I didn't really understand what I was feeling, nor did I talk about it with anyone. Back then, I had an inkling that this wasn't right or normal...girls are supposed to like boys, right? No one talked about sexuality or made it feel safe to discuss it. Even if there were others in school who struggled with it, I didn't know anything. Somehow, being in a Christian mission school made it even more apparent that same-sex attractions (SSA) were a huge taboo. So I stuffed those feelings inside, and went about life.

After I accepted Christ, I stumbled across passages in the Bible that made me realize that homosexual expression was something God "despised". Being a teenager, however, I felt like I had so many issues to worry about and interests to pursue other than my sexuality. I also struggled with my identity as a person and as a Christian. Life was consumed by the need to do well in school. I pursued my interest in art and that became a refuge of sorts for me to process everything. I also learnt the guitar and served in the worship ministry at church. I am really thankful for the gifts of art and music that allow me to express myself.

Even so, the sad, difficult issue of how to reconcile the part of me that is attracted to women with what God and the church thought still daunted me. The Presbyterian church I attended was openly firm in its stance in the very few times they had a sermon about sexuality and marriage. While a firm stance was definitely crucial, what I got from these messages was that SSA or the LGBTQ community were topics Christians should just not concern themselves with or be a part of. To my teenage mind, that was just a big NO, and no questions asked. I felt ashamed of myself. Once again, I felt alone in my struggle and did not know who I could talk to who wouldn't judge me for what I felt. Then, I was only beginning to understand and was barely able to articulate what I was going through.

Alongside my misunderstandings with the church, I grew to feel hypocritical and judgemental. I wanted the church to be a safe place where I could be myself and freely share my struggles. I thought that was what church should be, but I soon realized that the reality just didn't match up to my expectations. I wasn't able to share this part of me that I was deeply struggling with, so after 3 years, I left church for good because it was easier to reject church than to be openly rejected by it. At that point, I already felt deeply undeserving of being called a Christian. With a distorted view of God in mind, I felt that I was not what God wanted.

I still believed in God, somewhat. Even though I struggled with going back to church, I couldn't shake God out of my head and heart. In university I fell into a toxic relationship with a female classmate, but came out of that relationship a year later, after which I felt even more worthless. Through it all, I kept questioning God, faith, and my identity. I questioned God for hating people who didn't fit in His order of things. It seemed as though God favoured straight people. I was hungry for the truth.

> Even though I struggled with going back to church, I couldn't shake God out of my head and heart.

For two to three years after that relationship, even though I had been hurt badly by it, I was still quite convinced that all forms of romantic relationships were legitimate as long as they were rooted in mutual commitment and love to each other. Through these struggles however, God continued to speak to me of His love through various Christians I met along the way. Though I continue to wrestle with fully receiving His promises that He still loves me, these are the little things that have accompanied my journey of seeking grace and truth, and they have mattered a lot.

After all this, how did I come to accept God's truth about

His order of creation? Even though, in my experience, churches didn't know how to walk with me when I struggled with sexuality and more, God continued to plant various Christians from other churches, even from other countries, to speak His truth and love to me. I am privileged to have met mature Christian friends who did not shun me, but stayed and even shared openly about their own struggles to show me that I'm not alone. One day, I happened to come across an article by John Piper on God's order of creation and immediately I was surprised that I did not cringe but, instead, I read it with a strange peace and understanding. In His timing, I came to terms with the whole issue of God's order of creation. I don't think it was possible for anyone to indoctrinate me with these ideas, but it was God's Spirit who helped me understand.

In retrospect, what I feel might have helped me back when I was struggling badly was if the church had taken more time to recognize our collective brokenness and need for God, acknowledging those in the congregation who feel that their sexuality is a large part of their identity, or who are in the process of coming to terms with God's order of creation. Just the act of acknowledging that we have not dealt with this matter well, or that we don't know how to help or walk with those in need, could be a really important step in better loving those who are falling through the gaps. In calling for more grace and help to do so, we recognize our common humanity and God's sovereignty in our lives.

> *"And we know that all things work together for good to those who love God, to those who are the called according to His purpose."*
> *Romans 8:28*

I can affirm with confidence that what God is doing in my life is truly for good ... even when this good doesn't feel like that to me now. Honestly, I wish I could say that these feelings are gone forever because then I would have one less "thing" to deal with, but they are not. I am still attracted to women, and I'm learning to be ok with that because it's probably there for a reason. God is not trying to turn me straight. Rather, He is asking me not to resist Him, and He has been so patient. I feel largely at peace with where I am, and there is a greater sense of freedom that I am not bound by my ideas of what my identity is. The struggles are real. But I can breathe, serve people, make art, and live in that abundant life Jesus came to give. If you, the reader, are going through what I have struggled with, I would like you to know that, really, you aren't alone and God is still walking with you, even when it seems like the church is unable to. Your journey with God is uniquely yours, as is mine. But I pray that the church will learn to walk with us, even when it is awkward and difficult, because that's why Jesus came.

Grace Ho

MADE IN THE IMAGE OF GOD

I have been struggling with same-sex attraction (SSA) since 2000. I was not a Christian for most of my journey, and only came to know Christ in 2010. Through the years, I have experienced depression and suicidal thoughts just thinking about who, or even what, I am. There has also been no one whom I felt I could talk to regarding my struggles as I have been afraid of how my friends and family would look at me if I told them.

My first realisation that I was attracted to other men was when I was about 14. I was reading in a common area when another student walked by without his shirt on. I caught myself staring at him as he walked by. As my eyes followed him down the short hallway, my mind was thinking, "Wow, he's hot". It was only when he walked past a bend where I could no longer see him that I made the connection between the word "gay" and my thoughts. I had known that the words gay and lesbian described people who liked others of the same sex. I did not think of myself as being gay until that moment. I was clearly aroused in a way I had never felt before and my first experience was when I was looking at another man. "Am I gay?" I asked myself. I was confused because I always wanted to be normal like everyone else—to fall in love with a girl, get married and settle down. Yet, now, I was feeling attracted to a guy instead, not to any of the girls in school. I had difficulty reconciling the SSA that I felt with my own dream to settle down with a girl.

I did not tell my family of my struggles for two main reasons. One, my parents were conservative and did not talk about sex or relationships at home. How was I to tell them that I liked other men and that I might not be able to settle down with a wife and bear children? Two, I was also afraid of how they would look at me. Would I be worthless in their eyes since I could no longer "carry on the family name"?[1] I wished so strongly that the attraction would be a passing feeling, a one-time event, and that it would go away soon. Instead, I became more curious about other men and I would stay longer in the toilet just to watch other classmates change. In order to prove to myself that I was not gay, I tried forcing myself to have a girlfriend in school. I thought that if I was at least bisexual, I could hide the gay part of me. Unfortunately, I was not successful in getting a girlfriend and I took the rejection as a sign that I was never meant to be with a girl.

In order to hide my SSA from family and other friends, I had to put up a false front. When people around me were talking about relationships, I would often say that some girls were not my type and I had high standards. That kept me safe from the pressure of having to have a relationship with a girl, especially during my polytechnic days. My urges remained, however. I would always feel aroused when I looked at a man I was attracted to rather than to a woman whom many other guys would think was pretty.

During this time, I buried my thoughts in online gaming. Instead of thinking about gay relationships, I spent most of my time playing games and in school. My excuses were

---

1   Chinese society is patrilineal, so children inherit the father's family name.

also sufficient to prevent my friends from asking if there was any girl that I fancied and pressuring me to have a girlfriend. All I focused on was not being seen as gay by other people. I also practised not staring at other men for too long. This helped during my national service. Most of the time, I would be too tired from the basic military training (BMT) and I would not be staring at the other recruits. I was also assigned to an office role shortly after BMT, so I did not have to stay in the camp and risk having my desires and actions exposed to other people around me.

It was only during my undergraduate studies that things took a turn for the worse. I was still playing online games to keep my mind occupied with other things, but I came across a group of local players who met regularly outside and I joined them. There was one player who not only played well, but looked good as well. His name was Kelvin. I was attracted not only to his physical body, but to him as a person. I remember describing him, to some close friends online, as an older brother (although he's younger than me by a few months), and how he was hot and cool at the same time. I enjoyed his company, both online and offline, but I soon became attached to him emotionally. I started feeling upset whenever he participated in an event without me, or if he picked someone else to be his on his team instead. To me, it felt like a rejection. I hung on tighter, began to stalk him, and would wake up at ungodly hours so that I could play with him or hang out. I was so deep into my feelings for him that I thought that I would never be free from being gay. As much as I did not want to be associated with the label, I was still attracted to and aroused by men. I started to think that if this is how I am wired physiologically, then perhaps I really was gay and there would be no way to change it.

As I started clinging on to Kelvin tighter, he started to avoid me. I did not see it as him feeling uncomfortable around me. I thought that he was really busy or unable to take my calls, so I sent more messages and left more missed calls, until a point came when he did not reply for two whole days. I could not reach him online or offline and my heart felt heavy. I started asking "Why?" even though there was no real way to find out. Our other friends were either unable to tell me what had happened to him or did not know anything at all and there was also no way for me to pry the information out of them.

I started feeling depressed at home, becoming easily irritable. In order to hide my relationship from my family members, I had to hold back my irritation. I tried to excuse myself from family gatherings and spent most of my time in school, where there were friends I felt comfortable with. However, two days became four, and soon one week had passed without any contact from Kelvin. The feelings of rejection grew stronger and I began to wonder if it could have been my fault.

Other friends who began to notice his absence and mine started asking me what was wrong, since we were both quite close at the beginning. That added pressure on me as I knew I could not answer truthfully about how things had turned out this way. I could not hold the feelings in anymore, so I decided to open up to a few other online friends whom we both knew. They were the next closest people I could rely on and hopefully they could understand where I was coming from. I remember talking about how miserable and useless I felt, being rejected over and over, by both men and women. My friends tried to offer solace and comfort, but they were unable to help me cope with my feelings of SSA nor be rid of it. I was tired of being gay, in a state where I did not want to be. I wanted to escape from all of this confusion. I told my friends over a drink that I was considering suicide to end it all.

There were only two real reasons that stopped me from committing suicide immediately. I was heading a project group in my final year of undergraduate studies and I did not want to feel like I had abandoned them to work things out on their own, so I would only end my life after we had finished the project. Also, I wanted to give myself one last attempt at having a relationship with a girl. I liked a girl called Ariel in my project group and this thought gave me a sense of hope that I could be bisexual instead of gay, even though the attraction was not as strong as my feelings toward Kelvin or other men. Nevertheless, these two reasons prevented me from taking my life for two months.

As a result of the rejection I felt from Kelvin and the hurt I felt at not being able to even catch him online, I retired from online gaming and devoted my time to completing the project. During this time, I also started to find out more about Ariel. I found out that she was a Christian and that the small group of friends that we hung out with in school were also Christian. I heard from other friends that Christians were not allowed to have relationships with non-Christians, so I decided that I would learn more about God first, before I did anything else. It was close to Easter and Ariel had invited me and two other classmates to a church event. If anyone else had invited me at that time, I would have declined as I had not sorted out my feelings yet. They were simply just buried. But since I had decided to give myself a shot at starting a relationship with her, I accepted her invitation. It was the first time I had ever attended a church service and I knew that I would never have attended it alone. During the altar call at the end of the event, she asked gently if I would like to accept Christ, but I told her "not yet". I did not know how to feel about all of it yet as I was still in the middle of a depression and grappling with my internal struggles.

As my project was still some time from completion, I sought help from another friend, Heath, whom I had met online in the same game and whom I knew was Christian. Heath already had an idea of what had happened between Kelvin and me, since we all played the same game, so I felt more comfortable talking to him about Ariel as well. He invited me to meet his pastor during a private Bible study session so that my questions could be answered. I took up Heath's offer and went along, not knowing what to expect. They were reading through a book titled "Experiencing God". His pastor handed me a copy and told me to simply flip through and follow the conversation if I could, and that I was free to ask questions any time during the session. I silently followed them from page to page until the book showed a long list of how characters in the Bible described God. It was during that time when several descriptions stood out to me, such as "Comforter in sorrow", "my friend", "our Father" and "Prince of Peace", to name a few. At that time, I felt a peace I had never felt before, a presence that I had never encountered. Tears of relief started flowing from my eyes and I wanted to find out more about this feeling. I decided

> At that time, I felt a peace I had never felt before, a presence that I had never encountered.

to follow the indescribable peace and attended Heath's church more regularly. I felt safe at the church because although Heath and his pastor knew about my SSA issues, I continued to feel welcome there. My being gay and my SSA struggles did not seem to stop them from accepting me as part of their community. I started feeling less depressed and decided against suicide. The time between my initial suicidal thought and giving up suicide was about seven weeks.

I did not accept Christ as my Lord and Saviour until a few months later, and things did not simply get rosy just because I did. Ariel declined the relationship but was happy that I had become a Christian and we still remained as friends who could meet up occasionally without feeling awkward. However, I still struggled with my attraction towards men and I started having the same feelings towards Heath that I had for Kelvin. I was getting more and more interested in seeing Heath without his shirt on, and he was clearly uncomfortable with it. I knew how it felt to keep it all to myself, so I decided to be open about it this time. Again, it did not turn out well. Heath was not sure how to handle the issue and we both felt awkward whenever we met. Our pastor helped to mediate, but to no avail.

I took our pastor's advice to see a professional therapist regarding my issues. He provided a contact for me, and assured me that the therapist was an ex-pastor. During the therapy sessions, I learned the roots of my behaviour and how my past environment had had an effect on me. I never correlated my upbringing to my current situation and thought being gay was simply how I was wired. I continued to struggle with how I could have ended up in the same situation (vis-à-vis Heath and Kelvin), especially when things were starting to look better. I prayed about how it could turn out better, I prayed for the relationship to be restored, I prayed to be zapped free from the gay gene. I was angry with myself so I also thought about what I had to do in order to make amends and how to restore the relationship between Heath and myself. My pastor thought otherwise. Not that he was uninterested, but my emotional well-being was his priority. He encouraged me to undergo spiritual healing and to get connected with a support group instead.

As I prayed with my pastor, God was also slowly answering my prayers, telling me how I had to stop seeing myself as a victim and how I had to learn to let go instead of clinging too tightly. It is still not an easy journey, even now. I still think about Heath and Kelvin, my eyes still wander toward men I find attractive. I still get aroused by men much more than women, and I still have old habits from before I became a Christian that I need to break. But at least now I know who I am; a man made in the image of God, not gay or bisexual or any other man-made label. I am a child of God, not a victim of circumstance. I know that God has set me in a special place where I can be close to Him, and I know that God is there not only to accept me as I am, but to help me transform into someone better, free from the bondages and struggles that I am now facing.

Joseph Ng

RETURNING TO THE FOUNT

grew up in the '70s living in a three-room flat. Our small nuclear family of four included my parents, my sister and me. I remember fun, early memories of play at kindergarten and primary school. My memories of home life, however, were sadly different. My parents were often quarrelling or engaged in cold wars. As a result, my dad would return home from work late at night, staying out after work with friends. Often, my mum would be bitter and would complain to me and my sister that my dad was useless and that we must not be like him. All this sank into my mind at that young age and so I thought very poorly of my dad.

My mum would try to find her own pleasures in life through mahjong or card-playing sessions at home or at her female friends' homes. When her friends came to our home for mahjong sessions, I would be surrounded by women. Her friends would also sometimes crack crude jokes about men and women. I therefore became familiar with an all-woman environment. When my mother went to her friends' homes to gamble, I would return home from school on my own, becoming one of what are known as "latchkey" children.

I was academically oriented and loved reading books, which also happens to be a preoccupation of many girls. I therefore found myself gravitating toward to the girls in discussions about books. Also, it was during this time

(Primary 4) that some boys in my class started calling me names like "girlish" and "sissy". A few of them seemed to really hate me and would bully me almost daily. I concluded that I must be particularly bad or evil or worthy of hatred because otherwise I would not be called names and hated so much. I tried hard to fight back, both verbally and physically, but I just couldn't overcome the sheer force of their numbers and their cutting words. I remember then going to school with deep dread and fear each day. My family, being submerged in constant rivalry (my dad and mum, my sister and I), was not able to help me to address these bullies.

I discovered worse things about myself as I trudged through primary school—I was attracted to the boys who were sporty, unruly, and popular. One of them became good friends with me. The friendship turned ugly when he started to constantly chase me around, treating it as fun. On occasion, he would even press me down and place his lips onto mine. Unfortunately, I was unable to fend off such attacks.

Then in the '80s, I was exposed to my sister's romantic novels which had cover photos of good-looking guys with unbuttoned shirts, and they were muscular and rugged, with girls swooning or lying meekly on their chests. These novels would also have graphic descriptions of sexual encounters between these ladies and the male lead characters. As I was at the age of puberty, reading these books brought a great surge of sexual arousal. It was at this time too that I learned about masturbation and fantasies from my friends. The masturbation episodes quickly became addictive for me as I played out in my mind the wild sexual episodes between these powerful, macho men and their swooning ladies. As I was fearful and anxious most of the time, I would escape into these masturbation and fantasy episodes to relieve my tensions. These habits turned into addictions in my secondary school days as I had to steer through my anxious, fearful, and often shameful feelings of self. The media and entertainment environment in Singapore in the '80s and '90s was also starting to be very influenced by the West, with constant portrayals of sex or semi-nudity on movie screens, magazines, and newspapers. All of this fed my unhealthy and unrealistic mindset about masculinity.

As I moved into junior college, I withdrew deeper into myself due to shame over my same-sex attractions (SSA) and obsessive masturbation. I started having lots of condemning thoughts that accused me of being perverse and abnormal. Fears and depressive bouts of melancholy frequently afflicted me. I started to become extremely fearful of people around me and would imagine them always staring at me as though I was weird. I also imagined that others on buses, sitting in front of me, would turn around and stare at me for being weird. I started having suicidal thoughts often as I sought to end these pains. I would even pray to the heavens, crying out for a god of the heavens to deliver me.

Without me knowing, some of my college classmates, who were Christians, were also starting to pray for non-believers like me in hopes of reaching out to us with the gospel. Two of them who were closer to me started talking to me about God's love in Jesus Christ and passed me several Christian cassettes and the Good News Bible.

I pored over the Good News Bible like it was rich food

to my starved and famished soul. I would often tear up when I read of Jesus touching and healing the lepers, lame, blind, demon-possessed, and prostitutes, or even raising the dead. It was the first time I had encountered a man so full of love and power, commanding miracles and the weather, and having demons submit to Him. I also listened hungrily to the praise songs and music on the Christian cassettes with my Walkman then. I felt exactly like one of the outcasts who drew near to Jesus.

It was at this point that I was enlisted into the army (much to my dismay and fear) and also started attending my college classmate's church. Some church brothers who had completed their national service shared with me how they had gone through their stint in the army by depending on God and His goodness to them. Part of my follow-up included Bible study. I would cry often during worship in church when I was reminded again and again of God's love and kindness to me. I also started to have friends at church with whom I could share on a deeper level. A senior brother, who was quietly suffering from SSA also encouraged me often by praying over the phone and going out with me.

I was often intimidated by the army's physically gruelling demands. Due to my introversion and timorous ways, I was subjected to bullying yet again. Most unfortunately, I also allowed a male driving instructor to touch my private parts frequently during driving training. I felt extremely uncomfortable and often told him so, but he was manipulative and cunning in his words and ways. He also threatened me in various ways, for example by telling me that he would fail me when I took my test. I was ignorantly unaware that what he was doing was morally wrong. I was unable to fit into the biased, survival-of-the-fittest-loudest-and-most-powerful environment of the army.

God, however, remained sovereignly powerful when I started to correspond by mail with two female college friends who were then in the University. They had joined a campus outreach ministry at the Science faculty and they shared with me their joy at the discipleship they were receiving. I was thrilled by their sharing and, in a providential turn of events, decided to switch from the Accountancy faculty (which I didn't like anyway) to the Science faculty to join my friends and the campus outreach ministry. I was accepted into the faculty, much to my delight.

My present church pastor became my discipleship group leader then. God used him to start journeying with me through my SSA struggles. I became dependent on him for advice, sharing, encouragement, guidance, and help. I looked up to him as one with leadership charisma, love for God, an easygoing nature and concern for people. We ran into problems, of course, because I was overly reliant on one person to meet my needs for male affirmation, support and love. God started to direct me to learn new ways of relating, and to discuss with my discipler my wrong demands in relating to him. He was both accepting and patient in also sharing with me his own struggles, weaknesses, and inadequacies. God caused the friendship to grow under His Lordship.

My struggles with addictive habits of pornography and masturbation did not become better though I asked God to help me overcome them. I then joined a Christian support group where they facilitated support and prayer for Christians with SSA. Many of the people who came to the group had never shared their struggles openly in the church and thus all of us felt ministered to by being able to share our SSA with each other. The group was mixed, though, with various understandings of Christianity's view of homosexuality. Some were already evidently absorbing the pro-gay theology in Western Christianity in the '90s and bringing that into the group. The leadership was not strong and thus my group, which had a leader who was pro-gay, started to lead the group in that direction. In no time, the liberal theology started to spread, and many started to go into the gay lifestyle, no longer believing that God sees homosexuality as a sin. I was very badly affected and finally left the group. However, I was also away from church fellowship, due to the shame of my falling into the world of internet pornography and finally even into sexual acting-out with people on the internet.

I now realize that my understanding of the Christian faith and its doctrines/teachings had not been built when I fell into the regrettable sexual sins. I was badly affected by humanistic, psychological teachings in self-help groups which taught that sexual addictions were a disease. I also found inner-healing techniques that were of a psychoanalytical nature to be personally unhelpful to me. One of the self-help groups stated that we had to reach rock bottom before we could recover and that a relapse would mean a thorough acting-out of the sexual addictions again. Sobriety was an ultimate goal worthy of all our efforts to attain. Often, I could not reach these goals and thus felt extremely sinful or even reprobate. I thus strayed into the dark no-man's land with accompanying deep anxieties, fears and suicidal thoughts. It was then that I was diagnosed as having major depressive disorder and started taking anti-depressant medications.

In God's tremendous mercy and grace during those days of darkness, I came across more senior members of the Christian SSA support ministry which I had attended before. By then, they were no longer influenced by a liberal leadership and had even partnered in the starting of a new local ministry. It was like a reboot of my journey, though on a different footing. It was also here where I saw the leader, together with some of us volunteers, sharing at churches, seminars, and even conferences in Singapore. It was also then that I started to feel passionate about the possibility of testifying to God's deliverance for me. I started going back to my first church where my former discipler was now the pastor and resumed a discipleship journey with him.

In walking through this journey of restoration and healing, I have been deeply humbled by the pride, hardness and rebelliousness of my heart. The craving for love is deep but the insidious, sinful workings of the heart to "dig broken cisterns" apart from God's love in Christ are deep too. Yet, the gospel which saves sinners goes deeper to deliver and save through Christ's life, sacrificial death on the Cross, resurrection, and His intercession for His people. I am not free from temptations and even the sins that a deceitful heart can produce, but that keeps me continually needing to return to the fount of grace, mercy and compassion—Christ Jesus, my Saviour and Lord.

Jeremiah Tan

SEARCHING FOR GRACE

I have visited many churches before where I have felt that it was generally unsafe to discuss my thoughts, feelings and encounters related to same-sex attraction (SSA) with members of the congregation. As a Christian with SSA, I have always struggled to reconcile my religious convictions with my attractions and emotions.

For the greater part of my teenage years, I repressed the attractions that I felt because of the deep convictions I held on the biblical position regarding the expression of SSA. I did much research on the theology behind this issue and really needed to discuss this with pastors but never dared to do so. This need grew more urgent as I raced through my teenage years and felt that I could not sit on the fence without taking a position on dating, relationships and the expression of my sexuality any longer. In many ways, I felt left behind by my peers who went on to dating, marriage and having children.

I didn't dare to discuss my inner turmoil with my own family and other Christians even during emotionally desperate times. There have been occasions when Christian family members and friends discussed the LGBTQ issue with me while assuming that I am straight. Unfortunately, some of these discussions revealed their lack of empathy and compassion. Some would cite several Bible verses and proclaim that LGBTQ behaviour is deviant and clearly wrong. Regardless of whether or not this is theologically correct, talking in such a manner elicits an adverse response from those with SSA. In my case, I retreated further into the closet, but I do know that many others have left church altogether.

Many Christians are quick to assume that people with SSA will be helped simply by being told that the Bible says that acting on SSA is wrong. Yet, we see that in John 8:1–11, Jesus told the teachers of the law and the Pharisees who had caught a woman in an act of adultery that only someone who is without sin should cast the first stone. Romans 2 also advises against passing judgement on others, possibly because man's judgement is influenced by his limited perception but God's judgement is based on truth. Indeed, as the Creator, only God has a complete understanding of the complexities of the issue and His will for the affected individual's life.

Some Christians with SSA have studied the theology regarding this issue very extensively. Some even have strong convictions that the expression of SSA is against God's will. However, more often than not, these convictions do not change the attractions and feelings that linger and are deeply felt. Indeed, at this juncture, I find myself left with much theological knowledge, unwanted attractions, and plenty of guilt. Due to my theological beliefs, my own sexuality frightens me, at a time when I'm supposed to be accepting myself and growing comfortable in my own skin. I feel guilty expressing a side of me that feels natural and unforced. This is the part not addressed by the church— what comes next for Christians with SSA? Is it feasible to ask them to shut themselves away in a metaphorical monastery or deny that their sexuality feels right and true to them?

Christians with SSA form a minority group not just within Christian circles but also within the LGBTQ community. It is very important for the individuals involved that the church tries to meet their spiritual needs because no one else will. The LGBTQ community in general is unable to meet these needs. Indeed, many people in the LGBTQ community have scoffed at my Christian convictions because they view them as self-punishing and unfeasible. When Christians with SSA turn to the church for help, will they find grace in their time of need or will they find a place where they feel unsafe or ostracized?

Sometimes, I feel like the marginalized Samaritan woman at the well (in John 4). Interestingly, even though she had five husbands, and the man that she was with at the time was not actually her husband, Christ still told her that He would have given her living water. We all thirst for life, meaning, and fulfilment. Relationships can add much meaning to life and I often yearn to find my significant other. Unfortunately, I feel like this road is closed to me; I feel no chemistry with members of the opposite sex and am racked with guilt when I start something serious with someone of the same gender. I hope that members of the Singapore church can help Christians with SSA by journeying with them and letting them know that even if they never find a partner in this lifetime, they are still loved by many brothers and sisters. And even if they are expelled from their homes, they have a home in the church. May the church mirror Jesus'

> When Christians with SSA turn to the church for help, will they find grace in their time of need...?

attitude in fellow-shipping with tax collectors and sinners.

In a previous church that I was attending, many people in the cell group started coupling up, one after another. Anyone who did not fit into this mould was encouraged to mingle more and pray. Often, couples would selectively meet up with other couples to hang out and I just felt like a lamppost most of the time. I ended up leaving this church and it was quite upsetting to hear that some people did not realize that I had left until after a long while. I have often wished that my previous church could have reflected the love of Christ, who said in John 6:37 (NIV) that "All those the Father gives me will come to me, and whoever comes to me I will never drive away." Because of the strong emphasis the people in the church placed on marriage and settling down, I never felt that it was safe to say that my own set of struggles was different and more complicated than simply finding a girl to settle down with. The people there also created an environment where it didn't feel okay to be single. I felt pressured to settle down with a girl at a time when it seemed inconceivable. This increased my feelings of awkwardness and discomfort.

In that church, people rarely talked about their struggles, nor were spiritual issues discussed and addressed. Members of the congregation seemed not to dare to share a more vulnerable side of themselves and the usual topics of discussion were issues like problems at work. No one dared to rock the boat and share about struggles in their faith and personal lives. As a result, I felt stunted in my spiritual growth.

I wish that this church had been able to provide me with a safe avenue to discuss my spiritual needs and offer some mentorship and guidance. As someone grappling with SSA, I have often felt very alone in my struggle and without an outlet for expressing my emotions. Indeed, I have not spoken about my SSA to my family and many of my friends. Sadly, my own family has never been open to discussing this.

On a recent family holiday, I decided to bring along a book to read. In this story, a college professor named George loses his lover, Jim, in a tragic car accident. Grief-stricken, George plans to commit suicide. As he puts his affairs in order, his encounters with friends, colleagues, and students make him reflect upon whether life is worth living without Jim. This story struck a chord with me as I have spent much time wondering whether life is worth living without my own Jim. The poignancy of this story was, however, lost on my mother. One day, she decided to have a peek at what I was reading and did not like the synopsis one bit. Moderately hysterical, she confronted me about the book and exclaimed that the more I read such books the more I would be influenced by them. This angered me because what she said implied that sexual orientation is determined by choice. It trivializes a complex issue and says that the individual involved can wish his orientation away if only he tries harder.

I decided to attend my current church as the pastor and other members of the congregation have been willing to open their lives and share about their own spiritual struggles. They have even bravely shared their testimonies on social media and broken the silence on many difficult issues such as SSA and depression. All this made me feel safe about discussing my own issues without being judged. For once, I was able to open up to a community and reveal a more authentic side of myself. The pastor also organized a sharing session and debate on the SSA issue. These sessions were attended by Christians with and without SSA. Preparing for the debate made people with different beliefs work together. Talking about the difficult issues also made it easier to talk about the "easier" ones, such as divorce, depression, and greed.

In my own search for answers, I used to buy theological books on LGBTQ issues to read in secret. Now, however, it is no longer taboo to talk about it or exchange resources on the topic in church. I realise that even though many people's opinions on the subject have not changed, the open discussions have made them more empathetic and receptive.

In a time when views are getting more polarized and hotly debated, I hope that we will seek peace and pursue it. We are all sinners looking for love and meaning. I truly hope that the Church can help those on similar journeys to find the answers and reconciliation that they are looking for. We all deserve that chance.

Travis Wong

FROM "THEM" TO "ME"

II I'm pretty sure you're not straight." Those words struck fear deep into my heart—the months prior to this conversation with my church friends, the possibility of not being straight—of being like "Them"—had been like an open wound I was trying to ignore. For months, I was distressed by questions like, "Having an innate affection for people, how can I differentiate between romantic love and Philos love?" "If I experience the same kind of passionate affection for any male or female I interact with, does that not mean that I am attracted to them?" "Am I actually bisexual?" The more I asked, the more convinced I was that my attraction was more than mere friendly affection.

That remark had eradicated any remaining hope I had of being a normal Christian. I was a 19-year-old new Christian, and the thought that I was something so "counter-Christian" was just frightening. What do I do now? What will the church think of me after they find out, or of my parents whom they recognize as church leaders? Fear soon turned into shame and guilt that seemed never to wear off—the possibility of being seen as an outcast by the church was like a permanent stain on my skin that I could not wash off. Unable to deal with the overwhelming anxiety, I attempted to brush the thought aside. I did not want anything to do with being gay.

My attempts were futile. I found myself spending each day discovering new things about my experience with same-sex attraction (SSA). Gradually, certain mysteries started to make sense—I finally understood why I would always rave over the female protagonists in films more than the males, why I was so obsessed with my female teachers since Kindergarten, and why I was more into girl bands than boy bands. However, the more I discovered, the more afraid I became—there was no chance of denying that the *Them* had now become *Me*.

It took me two months to bring up my sexuality to someone. I was sharing an honest conversation with my pastor on my struggles in my Christian walk and felt a constant nudging to use the opportunity to answer some of my questions on God and homosexuality. Afraid of what she would say in response, I battled myself internally. About two hours into our conversation, I blurted out, "What does the bible say about homosexuality?"

She paused and considered my face for a moment. "Why do you ask?"

I started to feel my insides churn and my heart palpitate. I could not retract my question; what should I do? I timidly said that I would explain later—I needed time to plan my coming out in my head. "Why do you ask?" she repeated. "I think…I might be bisexual?"

Uttering those words threw me into a tizzy—they felt so foreign and strange coming out of my lips. Yet in the midst of the emotional buzz, my pastor gently thanked me for sharing my secret with her and reminded me that knowing that I was bisexual did not change the fact that she loved me. She ended the night by praying for me and entrusting my sorrows to the Lord.

On hindsight, perhaps it was God that had placed that question on my lips that night—it was His first prompt to glorify Him in my struggle with SSA. By using her to model His love for me, He started a budding friendship with my sister-in-Christ who would eventually journey with me in my struggle, till today.

Struggling as a Christian with SSA

As much as my first coming-out brought relief in knowing that I was no longer the only one who knew about my SSA, I was still clueless and troubled over how I would continue living as a Christian.

After I recognized that I am struggling with SSA, I felt like I was walking through a minefield every day. Not knowing how to contain my overwhelming affection for the girls I met, I resorted to chiding myself for days in order to keep myself in check each time I found myself attracted to a girl. I spent each day in anxiety, afraid that if I put my guard down I would unwittingly sin against my female peers. After a few months, I found myself loathing myself for having SSA and increasingly frustrated by how my anxiety had made me emotionally dysfunctional. I was unproductive in school and in my interactions with my peers.

——

I first heard of Wesley Hill when my pastor passed me her copy of *Washed and Waiting: Reflections on Christian Faithfulness and Homosexuality* (Grand Rapids, MI: Zondervan, 2016). Wesley's book illustrates the brutality of his life as a Christian who experiences SSA, but who has committed his life to obeying God's clear instruction that practicing homosexuality is a sin.

Reading Wesley's story, I broke down in tears. It seemed as though he had read my heart and penned down my exact fear of interacting with my sisters-in-Christ and my dread of never being able to quench my desire for life-long intimacy and companionship in the quest to remain celibate. For the first time since I recognized my SSA, I felt God comforting me amidst my anxieties and sorrow—"You are not alone".

However, when I finished his book, I was left devastated. Wesley offered, in one of the chapters, his insights on whether the Bible condemns Christians with SSA to life-long loneliness. The answer was no—Wesley summed this up perfectly in his paragraph:

> *"The remedy for loneliness – if there is such a thing this side of God's future – is to learn, over and over again, to do this: to feel God's keeping presence embodied in the human members of the community of faith. The church."*
> (p. 134)

Wesley was able to cope with the loneliness by building honest, intimate relationships with his church community. I could never imagine myself sharing such an intimate relationship with a brother- or sister-in-Christ. Apart from my anxiety over interacting with people of the same sex, choosing to be vulnerable and open about my struggles with the church had been a challenge. My attempts to reveal bits of my struggles with mental health and being a victim of sexual harassment had mostly been met by awkward silences; my friends immediately changing the subject of the conversation, or telling me that they had had worse experiences and that I should "suck it up and live with it". How could I move on when my anxiety and attraction pervaded every single moment of my day, even though I detested these emotions so much? The thought of having to share another raw piece of my life re-triggered painful memories of feeling embarrassed and ashamed whenever my brothers- and sisters-in-Christ disregarded the bits I had already mustered the courage to share.

I was also at a needy point of my life where I found it difficult to build healthy relationships with my friends. Haunted by my painful experiences with being sexually harassed, I found it difficult to love or trust my male friends even though they were not the perpetrators. I was also in a pattern of difficult friendships—while I found it difficult to receive love from friends, I was simultaneously also constantly disappointed when my uncommunicated expectations of them were not met. I grew angry with myself. Would I ever be able to form intimate trusting friendships with my peers?

My long-drawn bitterness towards the church eventually developed into bitterness towards God. *If You are displeased with me pursuing a same-sex relationship, why give me SSA in the first place? Why did You will the church to be a medium through which I experience your love, when my church does not seem to love me? Why do You bless the people around me, yet put me through such suffering? Was the Salvation given through Christ only meant for others and not me, God? Do You even love me, dear Lord?* God just felt so aloof and distant then.

Grace Transforms the "Me" to "Us"
Many months of struggling to pray and praise God later, I felt His gentle prompting again. At Wesley Hill's 2017

conference in Singapore, he placed the current attitudes Christians hold on same-sex relationships on a spectrum. On one end were Christians who struggled to embrace people with SSA and condemned homosexuality. On the other end were liberal Christians who believed that God will accept any believer into His kingdom, regardless of whether they are same-sex attracted or not. I found myself simultaneously at both ends of the spectrum—while I wanted to say "I am just made to be bisexual, God should accept me whether I pursue a same-sex relationship or not", I would also beat myself up each time I thought that way so that I would detest myself for being bisexual.

Wesley offered an alternative—to be in the awkward middle. While God's Word insists that pursuing homosexual relationships is a sin, justice has also been ensured by Christ's blood for all of us, regardless of our sexuality. Choosing to stay in the middle means two things. Firstly, it means a daily rejection of that part of myself that experiences same-sex attraction. This involves choosing not to meet my female friends individually when I recognize I have a desire for them, or pulling myself away from situations where I find myself at risk of giving in to my same-sex temptations. Secondly, it also means learning to resist self-degradation and accept that Jesus Christ has already cleansed me of my sins. I can now stand righteous and sinless in the presence of God. God was telling me "Dear child I know it will be painful, but this is where I want you to be".

God did not stop there. Amidst my bitterness towards the church, He sent three sisters who in their separate ways embraced my broken self and constantly reminded me of how valuable and loved I was in God's eyes. They loved me as a sister. But they also challenged me to be the church, rather than wait for the church to be the church. Ephesians 4:4–6 (NIV) reasoned this clearly for me:

> *⁴There is one body and one Spirit, just as you were called to one hope when you were called; ⁵one Lord, one faith, one baptism; ⁶one God and Father of all, who is over all and through all and in all.*

I felt God softly challenging me, "You are loved and valuable in my eyes. That is why I sent my son Jesus Christ down to die for you regardless of whether you are bisexual or not, and why these sisters love you. You have been saved, just like your brothers and sisters, into the church. You are the church. Do not be afraid, I will help you love them. Go forth and start building spiritual friendships."

—

As of May 2018, it will have been about seven months since I felt God's prompting to learn to forgive and love the church. In these months, the number of people whom I've learnt to be vulnerable with has increased from three to eight. I praise God each day for the love and joy I have received from these brothers and sisters, albeit after many months of wrestling with my mistrust and many disappointing attempts to love.

By God's grace and prompting, I have also decided to dedicate my life to working as a social worker with the Unheard in our society—be they the LGBTQ community, sex workers, migrant workers or individuals from Third World nations. I am currently a Year 2 Social Work major studying in a local university, waiting in anticipation to see how God uses me to shine His light and demonstrate His love to those who, like me, were once disregarded by their community.

Of course, nothing much else has changed. It is still a daily struggle to resist the temptation of pursuing a same-sex relationship, as much as it is still a struggle to be intentional in placing Christ in the centre of my relationships. There are still nights when the loneliness feels too excruciating and I have to text a sister to pray for me amidst endless sobbing. There have also been days when I give in to the temptation of feeding my SSA. However, with God's courage I have chosen to struggle each day in anticipation of Christ's return, when I will no longer feel lonely or struggle with my SSA. By God's grace, I am washed clean and waiting for the time when all things will be made new.

Naomi Goh

ARE YOU GAY?

|| Are you gay?" was a dreaded question that I feared answering when I first entered the arts industry. The irony: this is a community that is open-minded, and all-embracing. Surely it would be a place of refuge, a place with like-minded people and even a potential lover. Yet why was I so afraid of admitting that I have same-sex inclinations? I had ready answers like, "No! I had a girlfriend before. I'm just really busy. I don't even have time for myself. How to find a girlfriend?" at the tip of my tongue whenever I was asked any questions pertaining to my sexual orientation.

I'm a second-generation, Spirit-filled Christian, born and raised by a family of full-time church leaders who love the Lord with all their hearts, minds and souls. My parents love me and I have never been in lack. Like any other Christian parents, they would naturally trust that God would raise their child to be a straight, God-fearing man who would one day find love, get married, and have children to carry on the family line and God's work. They were right. To some extent. For many years, I lived in the secrecy of my own fantasy world. I found myself attracted to the same sex as early as when I was six years old. I was watching a movie on TV where a man and woman were kissing. Strangely, I found myself attracted to the man more than the woman.

As a young boy, I always found myself attracted to *Kor Kors* (vernacular for older brothers) and young men, be it on TV or on the magazine stands. When I hit puberty and went on to secondary school, I found myself attracted to many of my guy seniors. Being gay at that time was definitely not an option, even socially. No one talked about it. I had to be careful not to be effeminate because I would be called sissy or *Ah Quah*—both derogatory terms for guys who were effeminate. It was a harsh social circle but thankfully I knew how to butch up! I had crushes, but no one to confide in because it was unnatural and wrong for me to even be having such thoughts.

My first encounter with an older guy was when the internet came about in the early '90s. I was introduced to MIRC—an Internet Relay Chat room—where you could sign in and chat with like-minded people. That became my place of solace. I found out that there were so many people just like me. I felt excited, albeit knowing that I was playing with fire. No one knew. Eventually I met up with the first person, a guy in his early 20s. That was to be my first physical encounter with another man. It felt like suddenly all my fantasies were materialising. It felt liberating. But at the same time there was a strong sense of sickness in my spirit. I fought it for a while, but soon after, I had to leave because the adrenaline was causing me to get a massive headache and break out into a fever. I rushed home, took a couple of tablets of Panadol and went straight to bed. My mom wasn't sure what had happened but she didn't probe. I was guilt-stricken. Yet, I had enjoyed it. I finally could do what straight people did. I could have a potential relationship. But I still felt it was wrong. Regardless, that became the start of many meet-ups and my "yo-yo" Christian walk.

I had grown up in the church, serving wholeheartedly in various ministries—dramas, choirs and later, even as a key leader. But struggling with this same-sex attraction (SSA) was a liability and a challenge. I would be at the altar during every other Sunday service, or Church camp service begging for forgiveness and asking God to take these feelings away from me. I didn't want to be like that. Every Good Friday service, every Christmas service, and every New Year's Eve service were times when resolutions were made to become straight and rededicate my life anew. But it felt like God never heard these prayers.

I found myself going deeper and deeper. I had found a way of negotiating sin but still going to church. By sin, I don't mean struggling with thoughts and temptations. I mean having physical involvements with different men. I would get into relationships but, soon enough, would have to get out because somehow there was a strong sense of conviction in my Spirit man. I couldn't remain in sin. Truly the word of God rings true:

> "Train up a child in the way he should go, and
> when he is old he will not depart from it."
> Proverbs 22:6 NKJV

My parents had taught me all I needed to know about God. They had prayed for me daily. They had affirmed my sonship with them and reminded me about my sonship with the Lord Jesus Christ. In spite of my struggle with sin, I knew God loves me and is constantly wooing me back. But I was very confused. I became bitter and angry, as any petulant young man would. I wanted to love and be loved. I wanted to hold hands and hug and kiss. Why was I denied something that seemed so natural to me?

Over the years, I got to know many gay men and women who would share with me their struggles and eventually affirm that once I chose to be gay, I should come out and live the lifestyle; be free. I tried it in the Army. The irony: in a place where regimentation was the strictest, I found myself to be the most free. Perhaps it was because I didn't have to be accountable to church leaders or even be at church since I was in camp most of the time. The church was still a place where black is black and white is white. Don't get me wrong, it shouldn't be any other way either. But somehow, struggling with homosexuality seemed like a greater sin in the church than telling lies, gambling, gossiping or hating your neighbour. Homosexuality seemed to take centrestage whenever it came to discussing the deadly sins a Christian should not be involved with. So, yes, no one found out about me. I felt that I was the greatest sinner. I also did not want to shame my parents. They were key leaders within the church. I couldn't bring shame to them or to the family name. I kept everything to myself. No one (or at least they never asked me about it), save for three of my JC friends who were fellow Christians, knew.

I was in the army when I had my first partner. In all honesty, it felt like the best time of my life. We held hands, we went on dates, we stole kisses. He even stayed overnight at my place with my family around. To them, he was just a good guy friend and my parents did not question much. This was short-lived. One weekend, I found myself forced to be at Revival Service. My sister begged me to attend it, saying it was really good and not to miss it. I tried to avoid going, but couldn't find any excuses to give it a miss so I attended it. That evening, something broke. I was singled out by the guest minister (who is now a dearly loved friend and mentor) who said he had a prophecy for me. He spoke over my life regarding my call and purpose in the arts. He apologized on behalf of the older generation for stifling my creativity in the arts and asked for forgiveness. He talked about how God was going to use me to reach out to a young generation who were lost and even saw me in a stadium preaching the Word of God. He said that God was going to use my creative inclinations to serve Him and excel as I did so. While I was overwhelmed, I was filled with so much fear. "What if he exposes my sins?" Or "What if I get struck dead by lightning because I was currently engaged in an unhealthy relationship?" There was none of that. It was just a loving Father drawing back His son. A son that was lost, hurting, confused. He wanted to assure me of His love for me and that He was still just as interested in my life as He was when He formed me in my mother's womb.

> There was not a single altar-call when the Lord exposed my sins or shamed me. He dealt with me gently each time.

On hindsight, there was not a single altar-call when the Lord exposed my sins or shamed me. He dealt with me gently each time. I released my hurts and struggles to Him a bit at a time. That night I felt a release. But no, I did not become straight, neither did I suddenly have an attraction to women. But I felt loved, I felt a reinstated sense of sonship.

The next day, through a series of arguments, I broke up with my then partner. I was devastated. I remember wanting to commit suicide at that time, but my fear of death prevented me from doing so. I had never experienced heartbreak before. The Sunday of that weekend, I broke down in the car on the way back to camp. My family had no clue why I was crying. I kept mum throughout. Later, I texted them everything when I reached camp. I felt ashamed. I felt as if I had disappointed my family. I felt I had shamed them. But they were family. I had no one else to turn to. I'm pretty sure God orchestrated this so that I could finally come out to them. They wouldn't get to see me until the following weekend. Throughout the week, they would message me and assure me that I was loved and nothing had changed.

I know my parents did have their fair share of questioning God—"Why?" Or "What went wrong in our parenting?" Till this day, I can't pinpoint what went wrong. I don't know if I will ever find out either. Regardless, my family was all-embracing. I remember that we went for ice-cream and they asked, "What do you want to do about it?" They asked if I wanted to see a counsellor. I shared that if he or she is someone I know, who has been through it before and has come out victorious, completely made whole and straight again, I would be receptive. Otherwise, it was my battle to fight. Still, I didn't want to disappoint my family. That said, coming out to them and being honest with them was the first step toward breaking the secrecy. I didn't need to struggle alone. I found myself accountable to my family.

There was no miracle. I still had the same urges, the same inclinations for the same sex, and the same hang-ups. However, there was a shift—I now wanted to please God. I remembered the prophecy over my life. Subsequent prophecies by other visiting ministers also shared words of a similar nature regarding my calling and purpose. I remembered the immense love and grace that I experienced at the altar. I found myself serving a lot more in church on different projects, conceptualizing and creating shows, writing and directing. Putting life's experiences into the various stories on stage, I found a fresh anointing on every work that I set my hand to accomplish. It was the favour and anointing of God. There was a great sense of excellence on every project.

I found myself mentoring many younger people, contributing to the development of their character and their walk. God was fulfilling his plans and purpose in my life. But while God was at work, I was still very much susceptible to temptations. Being an actor and involved heavily in the arts meant that the heart was also often very vulnerable. I found myself getting emotionally attached to guys to whom I had become close. I wanted to always meet them and hang out with them. To me, these relationships were very precious. I've always had close girl friends. But never close guy friends. Not till now.

However, in my bid to keep these friends close, I found myself suffocating them. I was very fortunate, however, that these guys whom I was close to, loved me enough to speak with me and share what they were feeling. It was painful and sometimes even hurtful when they shared that I needed to back off, otherwise I would end up killing the friendship. It was difficult. Even more so when they started dating. But I learnt to give them space and to take another look at my unhealthy obsessions.

By God's grace, God has honoured every single one of these friendships till this very day. I have been their go-to for relationship advice; I have planned and hosted their weddings; and I am even the godfather of one of the boy's kids! God allowed me opportunities to share with these boys my struggles. I allowed myself to be vulnerable to them. I feared that I would lose their friendships and the very relationships that I really craved for. But again God was good. These boys have stood by me even till this day. They have been there for me through difficult times, are there to celebrate my every achievement and are there for my every performance and project. They did their fair share of research on how to help or care for someone struggling. Their first reaction or approach was always to love. Never to judge. I appreciated that.

Throughout the course of my life in university and later entering the industry, I slowly opened up to people who were willing to listen to me talk about my life. Not so much for sensation's sake, but because they were non-believing friends whom I wanted to build trust with. Still, I did wish that I could meet a like-minded believer who really loves God and also serves in the same capacity as I do.

Enter Linda. I introduced myself to her at a show that we were doing together. I had heard many things about her even before meeting her. She was described as, "she's exactly like you, only that she's a girl." I was intrigued. True enough, we hit it off really well. It was like we were old friends catching up on lost years. Of course, I'm sure, once again the Lord had orchestrated this connection.

One day, I felt led to meet up with her and to share with her my life's experiences. I shared honestly with her because I craved the openness to be myself and to have a fellow believer whom I could be accountable to—one who understood first-hand the struggles of being in the industry, negotiating God's standards and the world's (in this case, the community's) value system.

Linda never judged me, never once raised an eyebrow. Neither has she ever probed for more than what was shared. She always approached or responded from a position of love, correcting and chiding me in love wherever necessary. While only having known Linda for about five years or less, she has seen me through heartbreaks, hurts, wrong choices, and the death of loved ones. In fact, during a season when I made a possibly fatal wrong decision, she was the first person I turned to. I remember her rushing down to meet me, hear me out and pray with me. There was no need to scold or chide, but I felt an extension of love and hope and a desire to want to make things right. She exemplified such grace, just like Jesus did in the Bible when he mixed with the sinners and did not cast them away in spite of the strong urging from the religious leaders. He met their needs, expressed love, mercy and forgiveness and then always said "Go, and sin no more". Linda made it easier for me to share openly.

In that same way, my family has stood by me. They know my struggles. But they have never judged. It's hard to explain to non-believers who cannot understand why God can't accept gay people. They would say to me, "Eric, you know God loves gay people, right? You know that God wants you to be in a happy relationship with another man when you find him, right? I don't think God wants you to be alone for the rest of your life. God's not going to throw you in hell for being gay." Sometimes, I too cannot answer these questions. But as much as I have tried, as much as I have pushed the envelope, as much as I have tried to indulge in sin or even in seemingly harmless relationships, I have found myself coming to a dead end. A dullness in the spirit. Yes, I don't deny that there may be temporal pleasures and happiness, but deep inside there is an absence of joy. It's different from the deep sense of joy that I get from obeying God; from serving Him and seeing excellence in all that I do. The joy I get when I sense Him smiling over me when I'm in ministry, fully surrendered to Him. The joy that I get in playing with my godchildren and telling them about the loving God whom they can turn to anytime. Paul talked about being the worst of sinners and having to live with a thorn stuck in his flesh. Sometimes I resonate with that. There are times I ask God if this is my cross to carry—a struggle for a lifetime?

Though it may never be the same, I'm blessed with a multitude of friends and loved ones who will come to my aid at the drop of a hat. I have no lack of love.

There is the bittersweet feeling of love when I pour my heart and love into my two godchildren, thinking that possibly I'll never have offspring of my own or give my parents grandchildren. I'm grateful for my best friends who have made us family and my parents the godgrandparents. I may never find a partner of the opposite sex (as instructed by the Bible) but I pray that each wave of loneliness will be a wave that washes past and soon will just become a part of life, a part of the soundscape, a part of the journey of life that God has planned ahead for me.

Truth be told, I don't know if the day will come when I can wake up and say "Hey, I'm straight! And I like women!" but I know I will wake up each day purposing in my heart to love God more. To love His people more. To be an excellent steward of the talents and gifts He has bestowed on me. To be a good son, a good sibling. A good friend. A good godfather.

I will wake up each morning to know that His face is shining on me, ready to hold my hand to go through the day. And when I fall, I will remember to get up, not run away, but turn to the Father "Just as I am" and make right, dust off the dirt and continue running the race.

So, the next time someone asks me "Are you gay?", my response will be "Let's go for coffee and I'll tell you all about it!"

Eric Chan

YOLO

My life, as many people might perceive it, seems to be joyful and smooth sailing. I am outgoing. I am blessed with many friends and a close-knit extended family. Furthermore, I am a worship leader, head of the Creative Arts Ministry in my church, and lead a Bible study group of 18 people. I grew up in church.

I have two extraordinary brothers and, in church, we are affectionately known as the three musketeers. We are seen as promising young gentlemen and there are high expectations on us to lead almost ideal Christian lives. However, unbeknownst to most and beneath the optimistic mask that I wear daily, lie many crippling insecurities.

One of these is that I am bisexual—having experienced more same-sex than heterosexual attractions. I am not afraid to admit that this has challenged my Christian beliefs and adversely affected my self-esteem.

I had an acrimonious breakup with my first and only girlfriend one year after I ORDed from army because of irreconcilable differences—different dreams, goals and lifestyles. I was downcast and vulnerable during that period. To make matters worse (or better, depending on how you see it), I received a few propositions from charismatic and immaculately dressed men. They were charming.

Being the flamboyant and attention-adoring me, I succumbed to all the unwarranted attention. I basked in all of the love and attention but felt extremely empty at the end of the day. I vividly remember that I would cry buckets and buckets of tears in my bathroom back then, trying to reason with God why I had been stricken with such a calamity. A real thorn in my flesh.

One of my turning points was when I met a man; I shall call him John. After two dinner dates with him, he told me he wanted to start a relationship with me. I thought about it, and, while I did, we continued to go out. However, one day while we were having dinner, his mobile phone rang. He took the call and accidentally placed it on loudspeaker. I heard a lady's voice and, in the background, a disembodied baby's voice crying "papa". At that moment, I was lost and speechless. I didn't know how to react. After an awkward pause, I confronted him and asked him to come clean with me. I found out to my horror that he was married with a son. That was the last time I saw John. I didn't want to have anything to do with him. Ever again. I told myself that I didn't want to be with a 35-year-old man living a double life and in denial. His wife never knew about his secret.

This remained in my heart and mind for a long time. I told myself I would never again allow myself to be vulnerable to anyone at this stage. But, you know how it is. After a while, we tend to forget past grievances and revert to old ways—bad habits die hard. I became deeply infatuated with a girl in my class but that eventually didn't work out; yet another huge blow to me.

Months passed, and my flirtatious and fun-loving self again got the better of me. I met an army boy, aged 21, through an app and he was fonder of me than I was of him. Let's call him Jason. We went out for about six months; just the usual texting and occasional rendezvous when he could book out. One day, out of the blue, he asked me "what is the future of us?". It then occurred to me that there could never be "us". I told him that and he became exceedingly upset. He said that I was confused and a "F****N hypocrite". All this while, the main reasons I was with him were that he was convenient and I craved attention.

I found myself falling into a dark pit, reflecting on what I was doing with my life—living a double life, taking advantage of people's affection and attention. My life was in shambles. I was holy in church, yet behind closed doors, I had so many skeletons in my closet which needed to be cleared.

I still vividly remember the Friday night when my dad returned from Jakarta where he had been working for the past 13 years. When I saw him, I said, "Daddy, I… erm… really need help". We then proceeded to my room and spoke. I asked him "How did you manage to stay faithful to mum these 13 years that you have been working in Jakarta?" I thought that he would give the standard reply: "Well, I'm faithful and I need to do what a man has got to do". Instead, he replied, "Well … I did make that vow to your mum 34 years ago, which read 'till death do us part' and I am a person who keeps my promises. Additionally, I love God, and because I do, I will do my utmost to obey God in all aspects of my life. Lastly, all of you are my legacy, and I will do all in my might with God's strength to see all of you through whatever. Always remember that we have to walk the talk."

At this point, I hugged my dad tightly and could not help

but apologize. I also shared about my struggles with the men that I had gone out with. After hearing me out, he didn't reprimand me. Instead, he asked me if this was what I wanted in life. That question stuck with me throughout that night. I believe in living my life consequentially, which brings me to the point about Y.O.L.O. Yes, we only get to live once, and I should no longer continue sitting on the fence.

One day, I hope to get married in church to a girl God has chosen for me and start a family. Well … if that does not happen for me, I know that God holds the future and has other plans for me. I definitely don't want to be like John—living a double life at age 35—and Jason was right, I shouldn't be a hypocrite. I needed to make a decision and get off that fence.

It was then that I found my answer. No struggle is greater or smaller than another; it is how you deal with your struggle that matters. For me, I am more attracted to men. I have and will always be struggling, but I realize that, at the end of the day, I must stand firm on what I believe in. I am a Christian and I want to live without compromising the values that Christianity teaches. It may not be how someone else chooses to live his or her life, but this is how I choose to live mine.

I am in no way judging how you live yours, only God can. Regardless of whether you're gay, straight, single or married, at the end of the day, that is your choice. I struggle—still—every day. But I am convicted about the path I am taking and derive strength from my accountability partners, my parents, my brothers, my church small group, and God, to ensure that I don't waver.

There are too many ways to live in today's fast-paced, complex world. It is easy to be swayed in a million different directions and to follow every new trend till the next one captures our attention. I choose to live by my religion. It is my pillar of strength. Well, after all, we only live once so I want to walk the talk, and make it count. That is just me.

Jotham Tobiah Lim

P.S. I would like to thank my mum, my dad, both my brothers, Shadrach and Janan, and sister-in-law, Sheryl Cho, for their unshakeable support, for accepting me and journeying alongside me through all my highs and lows.

THE LONG WAY HOME

This is the story of my journey with same-sex attraction (SSA) for the first 23 years of my life. Even though I had been given everything as a child—faith and love—I remained dissatisfied and sought pleasure and comfort in the world, even risking my own health. God used my own recklessness to bring me back to Him, taking me by the long way.

Childhood

Childhood was a good period for me. I was seen as the golden child who enjoyed reading and cooking and had many unusual hobbies that were different from my peers. My parents expressed their love for my siblings and me equally, conscious not to have a favorite. My father had a bad temper back then, and when he was angry he let us know it. But on good days he would teach me all sorts of interesting things. However, once, he took me aside after church to teach me how to "walk properly". I went with it, but I think that made me doubt my masculinity somewhat, and I always had to prove to people I was manly enough.

In school, I was gregarious and outgoing, often seen as the natural leader. The only things I couldn't get into were computer games and soccer, which made me feel left out at times. But my friends and I would try all sorts of things, and once I remember dropping our pants in public as part of a dare. I had always been curious about male genitalia, without really understanding why. Around Primary 6, I discovered masturbation, although I didn't know what it was back then, and it became a routine during secondary school afternoons.

Teenage Years

In secondary school, I was very much into sports. I think it was an outlet for me to affirm myself as "straight", roughing it out in training sessions and putting in sweat and blood to earn titles. I tried to act straight in front of everyone and would feel sickened and personally affected when someone called me "gay" back then. I did not know that this was a term loosely thrown about in a boys' school. I thought my friends knew about my pornographic inclinations, so I worked all the harder to cover it up.

When secondary school ended, I felt jaded and wanted a fresh experience. I had a hard time adapting to what I perceived as a totalitarian JC system. Everyone was studying non-stop. Around this time, I started working out a lot more, and became a lot more vain. I tore my knee ligament after a sporting tournament and laughed it off, not knowing the implications. After surgery, I hobbled around for four months and that was my first encounter with depression. I tried to fill the emptiness by going to the gym and with smoking. My parents wondered why I was so moody but felt helpless to understand why. I tried to ask a girl out, and tried to be as charming as possible, but she was really studious and straight-laced, while I reeked of cigarette smoke.

I learnt to drink a lot. I had thoughts of suicide, and my parents noticed my increasing moodiness, although my dad thought I was being difficult. I soon got to know a girl in school and she was really friendly. We soon grew close and, before we knew it, we were "attached". She was my first girlfriend, even though I was struggling with homosexual inclinations all this time. I just wanted to prove that I was normal. We engaged in heavy petting almost every time we were together and I was highly insecure when we went out. Every date seemed like a show. We tried having sex but failed, ending up embarrassed and frustrated. We soon broke up.

I began to go to the gym incessantly and became huge, about 10kg heavier than I am now. I would wake up at 6.30am to hit the gym, and plan about six meals a day for myself. Even when I couldn't eat, I forced myself to. Around this period, I decided to tell my family "I prefer guys". This was the first time I prayed so hard. Over several days, I asked God for the courage to do this and finally found a suitable time during a family trip. My thoughts were that I should come out about being obviously "gay" because of the gay porn I watched. My dad's first reaction was to say that he would love me whatever I was. My mum didn't really know how to react. I was very certain I was gay and trembled with excitement at all the possibilities that lay before me.

Young Adulthood
I started my time in the army and threw wild parties for my army friends when my parents were out. None of my friends suspected my inclinations. I lived a double life, and I remember my first sexual encounter was after having had dinner with my friends. I told them I had work to do but went to meet an online date instead. The sex was so painful and unpleasant that I left the place feeling thoroughly unworthy and filthy. All through this, God was the farthest thing from my mind. I did not have a relationship with Him

as I have now, and I did not have an experience of His love. Despite this painful experience, the sexual drive in me was not sated, and I had various other encounters. Yet I was deeply unhappy and suffered a panic asthmatic attack one night. However, even though smoking seemed to be a major cause of the attack, I could not give it up because it gave me release.

I had many run-ins with my dad, who tried to suggest to me some kind of treatment to reverse the homosexual inclinations. I felt betrayed, but now I realize on hindsight that having a homosexual son was something he, even as a progressive father, could not accept. In my mind, I wanted to be normal and I tried my best to be so. I went out for a while with a girl I knew. We began to have sex regularly. However, she soon left Singapore for studies overseas and I cheated on her. I did not tell her the true cause of the break up then, but she told me to attend "Awaken", which was a youth retreat conducted by the Archbishop. At that point, I knew something wasn't right, but fooled myself into thinking otherwise.

I went for the retreat, encountered the Holy Spirit and was moved for the first time into making my confession. Up till then, God had been distant and legalistic. I felt thoroughly changed and vowed never to return to my old ways. Yet, having no companions on the journey, I quickly slid back into my old ways with another casual encounter four months later. I knew it wasn't right, but I didn't know any other way to deal with my needs. A month after that, I went for a Catholic youth event, where they asked the crowd to pray for each other in pairs. I told my praying partner I had no prayer request to share with her, because there was nothing left to pray for.

Interestingly, later that night I encountered a priest who told me he would meet me for coffee. I felt it was strange, but decided that I should be open, as with all things. I made time to meet him for coffee. He told me that even though I appeared to have many things going for myself, I had no defined objective and thus would end up going nowhere, becoming no one. He sent me a few verses to read regarding this. I was resistant at first, claiming to be happy with my lifestyle, for example, smoking. After a few more meetings, the truth poured out. I told him how depressed I was, how many illicit sexual encounters I had had, and made my confession again, feeling thoroughly freed in doing so. Yet he was wise enough to anticipate the mood swings, which came swiftly after my confession.

On hindsight, it was the readiness of the priest to reach out, to maybe even "cold call" a lost sheep, that made the difference. He could not have known whether or not I was struggling with something. But the readiness to listen and the direct care that was shown was not something I had experienced in the church prior to that. And the presence of a stable, trustworthy male figure really helped in me opening up a part of my life to somebody who could handle it. After this first return, the struggles with SSA still remained; I could not understand the reasons behind the unfair situation of me being a Christian and someone with SSA. I was privileged enough to encounter a counsellor who specialized in SSA, and he opened my mind to the different forces at play in my life, the difference between having SSA and being gay. He explained that although I was attracted to the same sex, this did not mean that I had to live a gay lifestyle. It was difficult at first, but I found a greater freedom in self-restraint and purity, in His will being done, not mine. It helped also to be in touch with other male community members whom I could trust, with whom I could share my struggles and who did not patronize me. There were also countless others who were praying for my return to the Father. Without them I could not have made my journey back.

A New Chapter
The sordid encounters and unpleasant emotions felt like a closed chapter behind me. It was as if I had stepped into the light at the youth retreat. There, I experienced for the first time, the joy and effervescence of living in purity, amongst the freed. It was a small intimate group, and although I did not talk about my sexual past, the joy and empathy were encouragement enough on the journey. I began to desire this heaven on earth, where people were good to each other, prayed for each other and did not use each other. Going forward, it was a time of blessing, with God introducing me to more and more people who were rooted in the faith and could pray for me even in school. I joined the university Catholic community as well as a church community. While these took up many precious weekday nights, they helped me in the formative stages of my faith.

The journey since has been one of self-discovery, realizing how insistently God loves me, grappling with the dryness I sometimes experience in my spiritual life, and keeping to prayer every day. I have seen so many positive changes in myself, from a gradual healing of my masculine identity to identifying aspects of myself that I had not seen before, both positive and negative. Along the way, He showed me how I was already a positive male role model and big brother. While my life could give positive meaning and energy to those around me, God also revealed to me the harsh judgements I had made of others, and the unrealistic expectations I had of people. There have been moments when the darkness overwhelms me, when I doubt the blessings God has given me or when I crave the temptations of old. Yet He always gently brings me back, allowing my restless heart to rest in Him alone.

After about two years of committed singlehood and much personal growth, I felt God's call to take a bold step forward to enter into a relationship with a close friend. I had thought myself content as I was, but it seemed that there was a bigger purpose to all this. After some discernment, I asked her out and she eventually shared that she was open to the relationship, and indeed had been for many years. We both agreed that this was God's call for us, but treaded carefully and committed ourselves to a chaste relationship. He has been faithful to us, and we see the fruits of this relationship manifesting as a greater love for one another and our families. Like all relationships, it hasn't always

> Like all relationships, it hasn't always been easy, but putting Christ at the centre has been our saving grace.

been easy, but putting Christ at the centre has been our saving grace. We always say that through each other, He is making us saints. His love is new every morning, and He never lets us remain stagnant in our love for Him or one another, always prodding and challenging us in different ways. As we look forward to the marriage vocation that lies ahead, we are reliant on Him to help us better image Christ and His Bride, to become the man and woman that He made us to be.

SSA was, and is, a rather awkward topic in the church. The general tone seems to be one of acceptance. However, although many want to empathize, they find that they do not have the vocabulary or the knowledge to deal with a person with SSA, even more so if that person is a loved one. The weight of having SSA is a tremendous burden that many young people have to bear alone; they have to find their own answers, and often get lost in the confusion online. The acceptance they crave from their family or friends is only to be found in the occasional homophobic comment or chance conversation. With little social support from within the church, it is only natural that they turn to self-destructive means of resolving their internal struggle. If only someone had told them that there is a God who loves them as they are; that it is not their fault for having SSA and that not only will they still find love, they will find the fullest of loves in this life.

Our tone needs to be the same as Christ's—neither belittling nor condescending, but simply one of love. When that love is preached from pulpits, and the actions of church leaders follow from that, people with SSA will find a safe space to come out and receive the acceptance they lack. This goes not just for SSA but almost any other hidden condition. Only then will our churches become places of love and warm embraces; a little more like the heavenly kingdom on earth that we are meant to be.

Gabriel Goh

GOING AGAINST THE GRAIN

I have always liked women. I shared my first kiss with a girl when I was four years old. She was a neighbour that lived a floor below me and was my playmate. We were playing pretend in my cardboard house and one thing led to another. That could that have been the start of my life-long attraction to girls, who knows. It was no peck on the cheek but a facsimile of a french kiss, something I had learnt while watching late night television unsupervised.

Being with Girls Was Like Being in a Secret Society
I have been dating girls since I was 13 years old and have not been single since. The adults in my life were not so wild about this. Teachers in school made it a priority on their to-do lists to hunt down little lesbian girls that held hands in their school uniforms in public on weekdays. My parents were devastated. They had been divorced since I was two, but they had remained friends, so they continued to jointly parent me.

I remember the time when my first serious girlfriend and I had just gotten into a massive fight and she had punched me and damaged my fireproof door. I had become very good at hiding but I could not hide the door or the tears and, soon, when my stepmother came home, she entered into an endless tirade that led to her telling my father what had happened. My father, upon finding out that I had a girlfriend, called me all the way from Germany at four in the morning to tell me that "if you continue with your nonsense, I will disown you and I swear it on my mother's grave". That phone call broke my heart. My mother called me too, but she remained calm and told me to stay away from that girl in the gentlest way possible; she did not say "I told you so", even though she had warned me from the start that this girl was bad news. But this was the beginning of a double life that I kept away from my parents.

This incident served to further my depression arising from my need for an intact family, i.e. if my parents were not divorced, everything would be perfect; if my father didn't have to go overseas to work, he would not have left me in the care of my crazy stepmother; if the girl I dated was a guy, my parents would surely be more supportive.

The Beginning of the Mother of All Lies

There was a senior who had begun to show an interest in me when I first entered secondary school. It was enthralling to be given that kind of attention. Soon, I received letters filled with lyrics of love songs and it made me so confused! What were all these feelings that I was experiencing? One afternoon at home, I called a primary school friend sobbing, worried about being abnormal. I did not know God very well then, but I knew what He had to say about these things from my distant encounters with Him during Sunday mass at a Catholic church I used to attend. But as soon as I returned to school the next day, these worries would fade to give way to being in a loved-up haze. I stopped going to church because of the guilt. Just when I decided I was going to reciprocate her love, she broke my 13-year-old heart. I found out she already had a girlfriend through her classmates who sat me down to tell me she was just playing me for a fool.

That led to my first relationship, with her classmate who became a martyr for me by getting into a fist fight with her because she felt I had been so wronged. This escalated into a series of other relationships. I was constantly trying to find the perfect person to fill the emptiness I just could not fill. I also became a serial cheater; before I ended a relationship, I was already cheating on the current one with the next.

Giving the Other Team a Try

In between, I dated a smattering of guys and the longest relationship lasted for close to six years. It was my attempt at being heterosexual or straight for my parents and I tried really hard, mainly because lying and hiding had gotten too tiring. Perhaps I was also trying for myself, giving myself a real shot at normality. But within my straight relationships, there was always a relationship with a girl somewhere in between. The guy I had been with for six years? I had cheated on him with a girl within two years of dating him.

A Victim of Circumstance

Being gay was as heavy a struggle as being a child of divorce. With both issues I never felt like I had a choice. With the divorce I felt like I had been thrust into a set of circumstances just because my parents could not get their act together. With being gay, I truly felt like I did not have a choice of who I was attracted to. Being with women just felt so much more natural and comfortable for me. I thought things would get easier for both issues as I got older. But the older I got, the more painful and empty it felt because of the hiding.

Being gay had also become my identity. I wanted who I

was on the inside to reflect who I was on the outside because that would mean I was true to myself and the people that mattered to me. When I turned 24, I decided that I was no longer going to hide—I was going to live "loud and proud" and I was going to find a way to tell my mother. I had given up on my father because I thought he had given up on me, so I decided not to tell him. I thought telling mum and her accepting it would be the solution to fixing some of the emptiness and unhappiness.

I had just graduated from university in Perth and I was coming back for a girl that I was dating. I thought that maybe being employed and being an adult could prove that it was no longer a phase, that I was serious about this lesbian business. This was not a lifestyle but an integral part of me that I could not deny.

Acceptance and Approval, Not the Same Thing

As God would have it, I did not really have to tell my mother. I was living on my own when I returned from Perth but, for a short time, my mother and stepfather had come to live with me. This was great, until my mother found that girl naked in my bed when I was at work. We did not speak about it until I broached the subject and it became my big coming-out story. It was a disaster.

For so long, all I had wanted was for my mother to accept me for everything that I was. I had told her that everyone else could judge me for all I cared, but I just wanted my parents to say okay to who I was. Of course, now I know that I had conflated acceptance and approval. Because my mother loved me completely, I expected her to also approve of my orientation and choices. At point, I felt so oppressed, hopeless, and unloved that I knew, at some point soon, I would punish my parents by killing their only child. I was filled with so much hate.

Life Breaking Apart at the Seams

My mother, after many months, came to terms with my being gay in her own way. She finally accepted my girlfriend, this girl whom I could see myself spending my life with though I did not want to marry her. I continued to despise the institution of marriage because I believed that all marriages were meant to fail. Still, a part of me remained deeply empty and unhappy. Truly, all I could see was what had not worked out in my life. Everything seemed like a giant mess.

Somewhere along my journey, I had lost three close friends within a short space of time—two to terminal cancer and one to a freak accident. It was heartbreaking to watch the ones with cancer die, and the freak accident was a great shock. It was hard to take. Everything just snowballed into a big existential crisis that I demanded answers to, but didn't know where to look for. I had come to really hate God. This cruel, egomaniacal God in my head just seemed to hate me. I spat on hearing the word "Christian" and severed my ties with this God I used to pray to every night to protect me from evil. He hadn't protected me, and He didn't answer my prayers. He took away everyone I loved and condemned me even though He had made me gay. How could this God say that my love was not true and that I was a bad person?

I was tired of living.

A False Light at the End of the Tunnel

Two weeks before I decided to kill myself, I was busy tying

my matters up. Among the list of people I was meeting to say my silent goodbyes to was the first girl that broke my heart, my senior from secondary school with whom I had kept in touch. She seemed different, so I asked her why. She told me about an executive life-coaching company that had helped her deal with her issues. I was intrigued and decided to check it out since I thought I had nothing to lose.

Unknown to me, the company's self-development pro-grammes had underpinnings of freemasonry and other pagan religions. For two-and-a-half years, I served the community as I would have a church, enrolling people to come find their identities and be in control of their lives. I was deeply entrenched in this community and no one I knew could get through to me. It isolated me from all my family and friends. I even broke up with my ex-girlfriend on the instruction of the founder of the community. I lost many good friends because they had insisted this was a bad place, but I would not listen.

A Knight in Shining Armour, Actually Just with an Electric Guitar

Fast forward a couple of years. Close to the third year in this community, I introduced myself to a man who had just joined the place as an intern, as I would have done with any other newcomer; except this one was different. I could not tell if he was interested but he seemed to talk to me a lot. At first, I was polite, but I soon became annoyed and indifferent. I had no idea why this guy was always in my face. We later became friends because my mother had said she liked him and I trusted my mother's ability to judge people's character. She had met him at one of a series of underground music gigs I used to organize.

This guy's name was Evans. We remained friends and he eventually confessed his attraction for me. I admitted that it was mutual, but we agreed that we would stay friends first. The founder of the community and his leaders repeatedly forced Evans and me to break up and we suffered verbal and emotional abuse for months because of our blossoming relationship. We almost broke up, but the concerted efforts against us paradoxically ended up pushing us together as a couple. Evans made a very convincing argument that I deserved a better love and that he would love me the way I deserved.

It took a great deal of convincing from Evans for me to leave the place. I just could not believe that such a community could exist to violently oppose God but be so deceptively good. I almost did not leave with Evans because of my ties to the place. We still credit this period for fostering our bond. We always say that the enemy knew we would be better together, so he wanted to tear us apart. We finally left at the end of 2014.

About two months later, I got into an accident which rendered me homebound. It actually turned out to be a blessing in disguise. It was the beginning of my coming back to Jesus. It gave me the time to read in depth about mainstream religions, and to realize that the life-coaching community had sold me a counterfeit salvation that had to be earned.

I decided to give the Protestant church a try and, the first time I did, we went to Evans' church. Lo and behold, there was a guest speaker who spoke about SSA. For the first time, I felt like I had been blinded and deceived my entire life into perceiving God as someone else.

Unequally Yoked but in Love

Sometime in November 2015, months after Evans had asked me to marry him, he decided to broach the subject of our being unequally yoked, a concept I was unfamiliar with. When he explained, I was furious because I still held syncretic views about God and I fundamentally rejected His authority.

If we could not align our beliefs and deference to God, we probably would have had to put the marriage on hold or, worse, break up. But Evans and I had already booked our wedding dinner for 2016! So, we launched into a gruelling four-hour apologetics debate, at the end of which I finally conceded that Jesus is our Lord and the Bible is our moral yardstick. I knew that if I did not accept Christ, it was only because of my pride and that I would lose this wonderful man to my arrogance. Evans had answered all my questions about life, homosexuality, dinosaurs, evolution, and the legitimacy and infallibility of the Bible. He said: "Homosexuality is not the worst sin in the Bible. Can you honestly say that you have never cheated, lied or coveted?" It was true, I had not even adhered to half of the ten commandments.

Coming Back One Full Circle

It took me a long time to write this story, not because it was emotionally difficult but because I had to juggle caring for my two-month-old baby while sewing the pieces of the story together. Nobody, least of all me, would have thought that I would get married and have a baby! I still have SSA, but I am obedient to God and grateful for my husband.

Now, my struggle lies in preaching a true Jesus to the

ones who think that our God is cruel and condemning, especially to the bestest of my friends who mostly have SSA. But I thank God every day for giving me the journey that I have gone through and for preserving me so that I may now vindicate our Lord.

Val Low

HE CALMS THE STORM

In junior college, I played the piano for Chapel. As the student music coordinator for the Christian ministry in school, I would organize rehearsal sessions and select the songs, and we'd practice until we were ready to go live. Those two years, I felt very close to God. Free. I was free to use my gifts to bring praise to the Lord, and be a contributing member of His community. It didn't matter who I was or what struggles I had. The Lord was calling; there was a need to maintain the altar of worship; and I was willing and able.

Junior college, however, was also the time I became increasingly aware that I was different from the other guys. I simply was not looking at girls in the same way that they did—while they pored over magazines, commented on sexy centrefolds, and discussed girlfriends and dates, I could not wrap my head around the concept. What did it mean to like a girl? Should I go on dates, too? Girls were simply pleasant friends to be with, and I could not understand what it meant to find them sexually attractive. I soon realized I wasn't getting something that every other guy seemed to feel intuitively.

Meanwhile, there were things that I was feeling—impulses that seemed different from the norm, but that I dared not investigate or identify. I had no resources to help me analyze my emotions. There was nobody to discuss my feelings with, nobody to tell me if they were natural or abnormal. I tried convincing myself that my crushes were just a passing phase—perhaps I was simply admiring certain traits that I desired for myself, rather than the persons themselves. However, years went by, and the winds of desire never abated.

University was largely spent navigating the conflicts and tensions that are inevitable when your inner self is severed from community, and when there are more questions than answers. Again, I did not tell a soul about these inclinations, since homosexuality, whenever discussed, was derided. I thought there was something wrong with me, and that nobody else would understand. Was it okay to look at guys like that? What if they found out? What if I was found out? I consciously avoided eye contact with guys I liked, fearing that they might find my gaze peculiar. Without confidantes, I suspected I was the only gay person on campus. I contemplated seeing a psychiatrist—I thought I might be going mad.

It was only after I had started working that I sought out the gay community. I visited spaces, whether virtual or physical, where gay individuals were known to gather. That was when I realized I was not abnormal. People like me existed, and they faced similar challenges in life—from the clandestine navigating of our identities in a predominantly heterosexual environment, to the dreaded perennial question of marriage during family gatherings. We conversed anonymously in online chat forums, protected by pseudonyms and a screen. Among a gathering of strangers, I found kinship, understanding and solace.

There is no benefit to being gay. You are constantly playing pretend. You put on a mask when you're with your friends, and have to conjure up opinions to offer when you're asked what sort of girls you like. It would all be so much easier if I were truly like the rest, instead of striving to play the part. One can't help not feeling what the others do; it's not a life one chooses.

Till this day, my sexual identity has been kept a secret from my family. I have also never mentioned it in church or to my church friends. Fearing that I might jeopardize precious friendships by revealing who I am, I keep the truth to myself.

At 14, I was approached by a group of Christians on an evangelistic outreach. That day, I realized that the Bible wasn't just about a bunch of questions to be answered at Boys' Brigade meetings: the gospel was the power of God unto salvation. I readily accepted Christ, began attending Christian meetings, and joined a church. However, in no church did I feel that I might be accepted for who I am. Sex and sexuality were rarely discussed—the bits that spilled onto the pulpit were merely plain, bare reaffirmations of the male-female nuclear family unit. Same-sex relationships were never mentioned, which added to my paranoia: was there a defect in me? I decided to move to another church.

The sermons at my second church were informative, practical, and thoroughly enjoyable. However, they, too, never explicitly discussed homosexuality: they negated that half of the discussion by reaffirming heterosexual relationships as the only acceptable model. Those instances, where they swept the issue aside with a two-second nod of approval towards the majority, left me feeling disenchanted about how they might accommodate me as a person. Eventually, I left because I could not see the community accepting me and supporting my growth as an individual.

It seems that in the eyes of the churches I've attended, gay people do not exist. Perhaps it is a case of sticking one's head in the sand—if they don't acknowledge the problem, it just might disappear. Perhaps they feel they can pray the gay away. Maybe it's just a passing phase— soon God will come, wave His hand, and awaken in the gay men a hitherto latent attraction to women.

I currently do not attend church. There seems to be no point. With their open rejection of homosexuality and their seemingly dismissive attitude, churches appear unable to accommodate people like me. While I still believe in Jesus, I doubt I would be welcome in any church. In recent years, the rise of gay-affirming movements has led to countermovements that seem to beseech, "Come back to the light!"

People like me might not feel that they can get any type of support within a church. Without acknowledgement that same-sex attracted individuals exist, a safe space for conversation and support cannot be forged. Perhaps I might have felt more welcome if there were a small-group context where these issues could be discussed in confidentiality. However, the current environment simply does not seem conducive for anyone to step forward. The suspicion is palpable: might the church be concealing an ulterior motive, to "out" us, shame us, or try and realign our sexuality instead?

Several years after I had started working, I caught up with one of my teachers from junior college. He tried to persuade me again to return to church and asked why I wasn't attending anymore. His persistence led me to blurt out in frustration, "I cannot go to church because I'm gay!"

There was silence, and then acceptance.

This teacher of mine is one I hold dear, and we still meet occasionally. It doesn't matter that he had never met a gay person before me and felt ill-equipped to be a mentor. What mattered, and still does, is that our friendship did not end with my reveal. Following that day, he has continued to meet up with me. He has chosen to keep pursuing our friendship, free from prejudice and clothed instead with sincerity. Up till now, he's the only Christian figure in my life whom I speak to about my sexuality. We rarely discuss this issue in particular; we often catch up about other things. But what's special about him is that he listens, regardless. One day, I told him I was seeing somebody. He didn't push for the details, and we didn't pursue the topic; I just wanted him to know that I was doing all right, that I had someone in my life, and that it was wonderful.

My partner and I are embarking on our ninth year together now. It's a relationship I've been so blessed to have. We've agreed not to have sex, which is quite unusual for gay couples—the gay lifestyle is very often about the sex, whether casually or in a committed relationship. My partner and I, however, have learnt to develop intimacy on a level beyond sex; an intimacy for the long run, where we learn to love the whole person even as we get on in our years. I've learnt to appreciate him in the way he speaks, in the way he smiles, in the little gestures he makes. We argue now and then, as with any other couple; but I've learnt from him the power of quickly forgiving and loving again.

Right now, I feel fortunate to be where I am. I'm in a trusting and loving relationship that still feels like it's on honeymoon; in my partner I have found an environment that's safe, and that I trust. I'm not so sure what's in store for me on the God-front, or where the Lord will take me from here. On some level I'm afraid of reintroducing God into my life: I'm afraid it'll rock that boat of what I've got going on right now. I must trust, I guess, that it won't be too disruptive. That it will bring more benefit than harm.

"God doesn't rock the boat," my teacher says. "He calms the storm."

*Thomas Tan**

* Thomas' story was ghostwritten by Karen Ho.

THE GOOD NEWS MADE FLESH
– Reflection –

❚❚ Listening. . . is a memorable form of love", writes the poet and Episcopal priest Spencer Reece.[1] That's as good a place as any for us to begin. In this section, we have "listened" to the stories of Christians who experience same-sex attraction (SSA). They have vulnerably shared with us their struggles and joys, their difficult emotions and hard-won resolutions. Each of these writers has demonstrated extraordinary courage. We ought to greet their act of boldness with our act of love, understanding, and compassion (Romans 12:15).

A few common themes emerged from all these stories. I wish to draw them out and invite you to reflect on how they present pressing and rich opportunities for the Church to respond. An act of love does not just entail listening. It also summons us to action. When we take seriously that "[i]f one member suffers, all suffer together; if one member is honored, all rejoice together" (1 Corinthians 12:26), we need to care enough for our hurting brothers and sisters to do something for them, so that in honouring their pain and experiences, all of us in Christ's family can rejoice together.

---

1   Spencer Reece. "The Road to Emmaus." *Poetry Foundation.* <https://www.poetryfoundation.org/ poetrymagazine/poems/54977/ the-road-to-emmaus> Accessed: 23 Mar 2018.

The Struggles of Having Same-Sex Attraction

Being gay is like playing pretend, says Thomas, for he had no one to talk to about his feelings, thoughts, and struggles with SSA. He hid his sexual identity from his family and church, for fear that it might jeopardize his relationships with them. I should know, having myself lived with SSA since I was 13 years old. This, too, is the story of many of my same-sex attracted friends. It's a lonely and difficult journey.

Christians with SSA also tend to experience a conflict between their spontaneously-felt same-sex feelings and their deeply-held Christian beliefs, as we see in Jotham's and Travis's pieces. They also worry, like Eric and Naomi, that if their SSA were found out, it would bring shame to their parents. Guilt is often thrown into the mix and is especially confusing to grapple with, since SSA is not something any one of us could—or would—choose to have. These feelings of shame and guilt are compounded by the often implicitly felt sentiment in church that, in the words of Eric, struggling with homosexuality seems to be a greater sin than any other sin, and it's a huge taboo. What are Christians with SSA to do with that? We didn't decide to have these feelings in the first place. In addition to shame, guilt, and confusion, a sense of fear, self-blame, and helplessness can also overwhelm us on a regular basis, causing us to want to hide our struggles even more from the people around us.

The Lack of a Supportive Church Community

The largest shared theme among all the stories is that the writers didn't experience churches as welcoming communities to share their struggles with SSA. It's a sad and sobering reality we ought to be eager to change.

Thomas found that the subject of homosexuality and the existence of same-sex attracted people were seldom talked about in churches. When mentioned, it was done so derisively. For Travis, such discussions lacked empathy and compassion. As a result, both of them not only felt there was no safe space for conversation and support about their same-sex feelings, they also did not feel they might be accepted for who they are if they'd told anyone about their SSA. Grace, like some of Travis's friends, left the church altogether. She returned later, but Thomas no longer attends church because he isn't confident he will be welcomed. I cannot imagine how this would sit well in the heart of Christ, and it should also bother those of us who care about His burdens.

What complicates this struggle is an over-emphasis on marriage from the pulpit. Travis felt that because singleness wasn't much talked about, he had to grapple with the pressure to settle down with a woman, something he could hardly imagine himself doing. For Grace, this firm stance on marriage sidelined any conversation about SSA. She felt alone in her struggles and didn't know whom she could turn to, lest she received judgement instead of acceptance.

This isn't to say that a church shouldn't address marriage. It must indeed do so, especially in a time when biblical marriage is increasingly devalued by our culture. But it should also devote attention to equally vital conversations on the beauty of singleness—not just by preaching about it, but also providing singles with practical support to enjoy a robust, fulfilling life in Christ.

Pastoring the congregation well in the area of their sexuality also includes courageously and compassionately addressing our collective brokenness—heterosexual or homosexual. This can be done by creating space for the struggles and questions about living out God's plans for the flourishing of our sexuality—be it an addiction to pornography or masturbation, emotionally-dependent relationships, pre-marital sexual activity, extra-marital affairs, homosexual conduct, gender identity issues, etc.

Further, when authenticity, vulnerability, and emotional safety are absent from a church's culture, it makes it incredibly hard for church members to talk about their struggles with SSA, or any struggles at all, for that matter. These were, unfortunately, the experiences of Travis and Naomi.

There are same-sex attracted Christians who, because they envision a life of loneliness and misery if they obey the biblical view of sexuality, seek out and believe in interpretations of the Bible that endorse homosexuality. Most of them do so because they, like anyone else, genuinely desire to receive and give love and intimacy.

The Challenge for the Church

The challenge for the church is this: what practices do we need to create that can make their obedience possible? How can a Christian with SSA experience a life of flourishing by following Christ? Can healthy (non-romantic and non-sexual) love and intimacy be found in singleness and in the church family?

Eve Tushnet, a Roman Catholic writer with SSA, expresses this urgent question this way: "What if we asked gay people who don't accept church teaching, 'What might make it possible for you to live out this teaching in a way that's fruitful and not barren? And how can we serve you and welcome you even if our sexual morality never changes?'"[2]

"Fruitful and not barren"—that's what would make obedience to Christ's teachings life-giving. Every Christian, including our brothers and sisters with SSA, is meant to experience His promise of an abundant live (John 10:10).

How can the Church be the answer to Tushnet's question: "What if gay people could find more forms of devoted, honored love in the church than outside it?"[3]

What's the Good News?

Thankfully, not everything from these stories is about the writers' negative experiences of the church. They also shared what was helpful to them, and these are treasures we can mine. We don't have to be bogged down with excessive guilt by their unpleasant encounters with the church community, but we do need to honestly acknowledge that these are indictments of where the church hasn't done so well. These indictments, however, are invitations for us to grow to become more of a gospel community to our brothers and sisters with SSA.

The experiences of the writers show us clearly that the church can't just preach on what God's Word says about homosexuality. It also has to practise the Bible's enjoinment to "bear one another's burdens" (Galatians 6:2)—in

2 Eve Tushnet. "Pope Francis wants the church to apologize to gay people. Here's what that could look like." *Vox*. 1 Jul 2016. <https://www.vox.com/2016/7/1/12070954/pope-francis-lgbt-apology> Accessed: 23 Mar 2018.

3 Ibid.

this case, by supporting people to obey God's design for sexuality. Pastor Corey Widmer carries the conviction that "any church that holds a traditional view of sexuality must also foster a radical practice of Christian community in which living out a biblical sexual ethic becomes possible and even attractive."[4]

If the church isn't the kind of community in which same-sex attracted Christians can flourish as they follow Christ, then why should we be surprised if they turn toward other kinds of communities—communities that seek to show them love and acceptance, and promote their well-being in their own (albeit non-biblical) ways?

Associate Professor of Theology Matt Jenson puts it this way:

> [T]he church is right to tell gay people the good news and call them to a life of discipleship if, and only if, it is willing to live as their family. If the church is unwilling to be family to gay people, it has no business giving them the Gospel. [. . .] When the church is truthful, when it lives out what it means to be the household of God, it demonstrates the truth of the Gospel. When it doesn't live this out, it bears false witness, no matter what it says, making it look like the Gospel is just what so many suspect it is: too good to be true.[5]

---

4   Corey Widmer. "Traditional Sexuality, Radical Community." *The Gospel Coalition.* 3 Oct 2014. <https://www. thegospelcoalition. org/article/traditional-sexuality-radical-community/> Accessed: 23 Mar 2018.

5   Matt Jenson. "The Church is Your Family: Reflections for Sin-

But we don't have a gospel that's too good to be true. We have a church community that's too slow to show the gospel to be true. But, by God's grace and mercy, we're not too late. From the stories of these writers, we can glean instances of how the church has been a gospel community to them.

Friends and Mentors

For Joseph, Jeremiah, Eric, Gabriel, Val, and Naomi, they had trusted friends in whom they could confide their struggles. Their friends provided a safe space for them to share their difficulties and questions, and lovingly responded to them with acceptance and accountability, necessary corrections and patient explanations.

Mentor figures played a vital role in the lives of Jeremiah, Gabriel, and Thomas. Each of them was blessed to have met a mentor who proactively reached out to them and wisely walked with them.

Pastor Brad Hambrick asks, "Think about your own congregation. If someone is experiencing unwanted SSA—and it's likely someone is—whom would they talk to? Where would they find support? What quality of honest friendship is available to them?"[6] How would you respond to this question with regards to your church?

---

gles & Those Struggling with Homosexuality." *Biola University*. 6 Apr 2011. <http://open.biola.edu/resources/the-church-is-your-family-reflections-for-singles-those-struggling-with-homosexuality> Accessed: 23 Mar 2018.

6   Brad Hambrick. "How Your Church Can Prepare for National Coming Out Day." *The Gospel Coalition*. 8 Oct 2016. <https://www.thegospelcoalition.org/article/how-your-church-can-prepare-for-national-coming-out-day/> Accessed: 23 Mar 2018.

"When Christians with SSA turn to the church for help," wonders Travis, "will they find grace in their time of need or will they find a place where they feel unsafe or ostracized?"

An Authentic Church Culture

We've seen earlier how the lack of a culture of authenticity and the absence of conversations on SSA were unhelpful to same-sex attracted Christians. A positive counterpart of this can be seen in the stories of Travis and Grace.

Travis found another church in which church leaders and members were willing to open up about their own struggles. For Grace, her friends did that with her. This made both of them feel they were not alone in grappling with SSA, and helped them to feel more comfortable in revealing their own difficult issues to their church friends.

What encouraged Travis even more was that his pastor organized a session in which the subject of SSA was openly discussed and respectfully debated. He witnessed how these conversations led his church to be more empathetic to the experiences of same-sex attracted people. Similarly, hearing a guest speaker share about SSA was a key moment in Val's faith journey.

Specialized Support

For Gabriel and Joseph, they benefitted from professional counselling, which allowed them to work on their deeper, unresolved issues with a trained therapist.

Inner healing was also helpful in Joseph's journey, as was attending a support group that helped Christians with SSA to journey toward holiness and wholeness. Jeremiah likewise found this useful. A support group sounded akin to the confidential small group Thomas desired to experience. One wonders if he would have stayed in church if that had been available to him then.

Saying "Yes" to Something Greater, Something Better

Reflecting on the stories of these writers and my own journey, I would say that the most important thing is for same-sex attracted Christians to understand rightly God's character and His heart for us, something in which the church has a crucial role to play.

Denying ourselves from acting on our same-sex desires can be difficult and painful, but if that's all there is to it, then obedience to God would become onerous and tiresome to us—a heavy burden that's unbearable (Matthew 23:4).

Rather, what ought to compel obedience to God is the understanding that self-denial isn't the end of the road, but the beginning of the path toward the abundant goodness God has in store for us. Pastor Nick Roen, who is himself same-sex attracted, expresses this well:

> What the church needs is an alternative script. And it must be a holistic script that accounts for the real emotions and desires of those with SSA. We can't live a life of only saying, "No!" to our desires. We need to be able to say "Yes!" to something greater, something better.
>
> The most basic—and the most glorious—thing that I have said "Yes!" to is Jesus. The joys of

following Jesus are everlasting and complete (Psalm 16:11; Mark 10:29–30) and make the temporary promises of sin seem woefully lacking. However, following Jesus does not make my yearnings for human intimacy and companionship magically disappear. What does Christianity have to say to those areas?[7]

What Christianity has to offer to same-sex attracted people are healthy and intimate relationships in the church family. Pastor Sam Allberry, who also has SSA, believes the church "should have the most wonderful and attractive relationships" in the world.[8]

In other words, what helps same-sex attracted Christians to follow Jesus is when the church becomes "family to gay people". Widmer is convinced that one of the church's most urgent tasks today is to create a counter-cultural community "that make[s] the demands of the gospel plausible, practical, and attractive. If a gay [person] is going to embrace a life of chastity for Jesus Christ, she [or he] must be able to look into the future and see not only the loss and pain but also the possibility that a real fulfilling life can be lived."[9]

---

7   Nick Roen. "An Alternative Script for Same-Sex Attraction." *Desiring God*. 20 Nov 2013. <https://www. desiringgod.org/articles/an-alternative-script-for-same-sex-attraction> Accessed: 23 Mar 2018.
8   Sam Allberry. "Homosexuality and the World." In: *Is God anti-gay?: And other questions about homosexuality, the Bible and same-sex attraction*. 85. Denmark: The Good Book Company. 2015.
9   Corey Widmer. "Traditional Sexuality, Radical Community." *The Gospel Coalition*. 3 Oct 2014. <https://www. thegospelcoalition.org/article/traditional-sexuality-radical-community/> Accessed: 23 Mar 2018.

Holiness is supposed to be beautiful, not burdensome. But that cannot happen unless the church supports same-sex attracted Christians in such a way that they can live full and fulfilling lives in their discipleship journey.

This way, obedience to Jesus would be not only possible, but also promising. Several writers shared that it was important to them to know that God loved them and had a specific destiny for their lives. Being drawn by the greater love of God for them was what compelled them to stop pursuing the lesser pleasures of sin and to leave the life He didn't intend for them. Karen's story illustrates this well. The church needs to embody these expressions of God's love to Christians with SSA in credible, concrete, constructive, and creative ways.

Our Welcome and Witness to a Watching and Waiting World

I shall leave you with the words of Mike Haley, a man who used to pursue his same-sex desires, until God met with him profoundly and called him to follow Him. Haley observes that a large amount of money has been spent for the work of missions, and notes that with this money, the church has:

> trained missionaries. We helped them to learn a foreign language. They will often study that language intensively for years. They will study the group of people that they are attempting to reach for Christ; they will find out the social nuances of that group of people; they will find out how all those people dress, so that when they become a part of that community, they won't offend them.

And I challenge us today: How much money, effort, and energy are we putting in to learning how to reach the unwanted harvest known as the gay and lesbian community?[10]

When the Lord of the harvest sends us to the mission field of same-sex attracted people, are our churches ready to be family to them or will they become unwanted harvest, unable to find a place in church to call home?

Raphael Zhang
Focus on the Family Singapore

---

10   Mike Haley. *Love Won Out: Testifying to God's Grace*. DVD. *Focus on the Family*. 2006.

SECTION 2 — WALKING ALONGSIDE

MY FRIEND IS IN GOD'S HANDS

Yen* and I walked down a narrow alley in silence. A few days earlier, Yen had sent me a text message: "I want to go to this clinic where you can check for AIDS...." He had gone for a medical check-up prior to messaging me and the doctor had raised something troubling.

We went, but were told to go back later—or it was the wrong clinic—I cannot remember. Leaving the clinic that afternoon, Yen was silent. And I had nothing to say. I prayed and hoped hard that Yen was not HIV-positive, feeling a great heaviness and powerlessness to do anything to help him.

A few years before that visit to the clinic, Yen had called me late one night. There was desperation in his voice. It sounded like he had been crying. I think if he had not been so depressed, he might not have shared what he had shared then. Yen said that he was upset with a good guy friend because this friend seemed to take him for granted and paid a lot of attention to others. Yen then admitted that he was in love with this friend but felt suicidal because that love was not reciprocated.

That was an unexpected revelation, but not entirely surprising. As Yen spoke, I realized that I had been carrying this fear for a while, that one day he would tell me that he is struggling with same-sex attraction (SSA). I do not recall what I said to Yen that night, only that I listened and did not say much, partly because I did not know what to say or do.

In the last few years of journeying with Yen and a few other Christians with SSA, what stood out for me was how little I knew about what to do and how to relate to them rightly. I respected Yen because he was always honest with where he was with God. I saw how, at times, he had faith and trusted that homosexual acting out was not God's will for him. At other times, he was angry at God, doubted God, or just wanted to not care or think about what God thought of homosexuality or of him. I knew that he hoped God might allow him the blessings of living together with a long-term male partner. Yen knew I subscribed to the orthodox position that homosexual acting out was against God's will, but at times when Yen was questioning and struggling with God, I often wondered, was I supposed to be communicating more of how his sexual acting out is sinful? Was I supposed to warn Yen more of the temptations of hanging around gay friends? Was I supposed to do more for Yen?

Looking back, perhaps it was good that I did not know what to do, because it made me listen to Yen more and empathize before giving any hasty advice or counsel. It gave me the enormous privilege of crying with Yen when things were hard, helping him come before God when he felt ashamed and wanted to confess sins. Aware of my utter helplessness to do anything to take away Yen's SSA feelings or make his questions, doubts and anger at God go away, I realized that I could only trust God with Yen. Praying for him was the only thing I really could do for him. What was not helpful to Yen, especially in the first few years journeying with him, was how I amplified his struggle with SSA over any other struggle or any other aspect of his life. I was also unconsciously comparing myself with Yen and concluding that his SSA struggle was greater than any struggles I had or could have. And this manifested in the way I responded to him on one occasion. We had agreed to meet up for coffee one day. But he had failed to confirm the details the day before our meet up, and also did not answer my calls on the day we were to meet. It was only a few weeks later that he apologized and explained that he had been really busy the whole day with work and, therefore, had not replied to the message I had sent.

My first thought then was that it was okay; after all, how could I hold Yen accountable for his rudeness and inconsideration when he had such big struggles in life to battle with? It was only later that I realized that, in some way, carrying Yen's secret about his SSA struggles was causing me to treat him with kid gloves, to expect less of him than I would with other friends, to see and treat him as a victim because of his SSA struggles.

As a result, I had also refrained from sharing much about my personal struggles and problems with Yen and did not let him be a friend to me although I demanded of myself to be readily available to lend a listening ear to Yen and be there for him when the need arose. Unconsciously, I had treated Yen less as a peer, a friend, and more as if he were a needy case God had assigned to me.

Journey Canada

That changed when I got to know of Journey Canada—a discipleship ministry that cares for people struggling with relational and sexual issues—while I was in Vancouver. As I heard brothers and sisters share openly about their struggles in Journey's small groups, I recognized that no matter the specific nature of the sins each of us struggle with, all of us have been wounded by others and are wounding others. And before God, we are all unable to respond rightly—whatever the nature of our sins.

What was more surprising was being convicted that *I* was not excluded from this. When I compared and downplayed my struggles and sinful tendencies in relation to Yen, I was conveniently turning a blind eye to all that trapped *me* from a free and loving response to God or others.

Realizing that, I resolved to treat Yen truly as a friend and a peer, someone who, like me, needs community and friendship but also someone who is responsible before God for all that he chooses to do or not do. As I did so, I found that I truly enjoyed Yen's company—beyond just wanting to spend time with him to help or fix him. God was enabling me to see Yen beyond his SSA struggle as a person with strengths and weaknesses, with traits that really annoy others as well as ones that were truly admirable and fine. I also started sharing more of my life with Yen, revealing my true self, and how I wanted to be respected and treated as a friend as well.

The problem with comparing Yen's struggle to mine and amplifying his struggles, was that it made me doubt that God could really do anything to help Yen. Though I prayed, I didn't really believe that God would do anything for Yen. It was as if I had more empathy for Yen's plight than God did. It was only as I increasingly noticed how much I also needed God to deliver me from my own sins and saw that God truly could and did meet me in my places of pain and emptiness, that my confidence in God's care and His ability to transform Yen grew.

Let's go back to that day when Yen and I visited the AIDS clinic. We eventually found out that he did not have HIV. I don't know what Yen thought of this outcome, but I am convinced that God did do a miracle that day and kept Yen from HIV infection. For me, that was a profound moment. I saw that Yen was and is in God's hands. And that God did care for him greatly and cares more than anyone can to lead Yen to Himself.

Also, knowing that Yen has had experiences that make it hard for him to deny that God is real in his life has helped me pray for Yen with more faith. I ask that God have mercy on Yen and on me, that God draw Yen nearer to Himself daily and that Yen, like myself and any other person, would daily live more and more into the life that Christ died on the cross for each of us to live.

Nowadays when I see Yen, I find myself thinking of the following: I do not fully understand your struggle and why God allowed it. I know this causes much pain, confusion, and loneliness. I do not know what God is doing in your life. However, I trust (some days I do and on other days, I want to trust this!) that whatever He does in your life, or in mine, is truly for good—real solid good that we will be able to "taste and see" one day. For now, what I do know is that you know God and you know God's voice, just as I do. So, can we help each other hear and respond to God's voice today?

Constance Chan

THRIVING IN COMMUNITY

As a greenhorn in the entertainment industry, I had heard of Eric* and how he was a prominent member within the industry who wasn't afraid to be open about being a Christian. He was a rarity in my line of work and I hoped that eventually we would get a chance to work together. Unbeknownst to me, he had also heard that I was a committed Christian and was hoping to speak to me about it. That chance came along in 2014, when we had to work on a project together.

In the second week of knowing each other, we decided to go for lunch one day to share more about being believers in our industry. Right from the get-go, we knew we could trust each other. We ended up spending about three hours talking about our lives and the challenges of holding fast to our faith in such a secular and liberal arena. We had many things in common—we both had strict Christian up-bringings, were actively serving in several ministries in our local churches, and were committed to remaining stead-fast in our faith and to bringing the light of Jesus into our workplace. Needless to say, Eric and I became fast friends.

Eric also shared something incredibly personal with me during that first lunch: he was gay. He openly and gen-erously shared about his lifelong struggle of coming to accept his sexual orientation, yet fighting against it in or-der to remain faithful and obedient to the Lord. My heart broke for him as he recounted instances where he had stumbled, and times of pain and conflict with broken relationships and family members who were struggling to understand his heart. I left our lunch that day incredibly saddened for his struggles, but also tremendously heartened that in spite of having gone through so much, he was still determined to choose obedience and purity for Christ.

Over the years our friendship has grown, and I have had many opportunities to get to know his family members and church friends. Eric and his family have always been wonderful connectors of people; they regularly host dinners and parties at their home and are constantly encouraging their friends to make connections with each other through their own warmth, hospitality, and generosity. They have a great capacity to love and to nurture, and it is through these opportunities for interaction that Eric's church friends have become my own friends as well.

I must say that I have been incredibly encouraged seeing how well-supported Eric is by his family and church community. He has many straight Christian male friends who are aware of his same-sex attraction (SSA) and are not afraid to remain close to him, in order to demonstrate how to relate healthily to other men in a platonic setting, and to show him that he doesn't need to be a pariah within the church community just because of his SSA. Eric has shared with me how this has helped him to remain connected to the body of Christ and encouraged him to stay rooted to his church community instead of seeking acceptance elsewhere.

Yet, I still feel heartbroken at seeing the extent of the loneliness that Eric continues to face and how he still battles against his desires to pursue a romantic relationship with a man on a regular basis. At times, this loneliness and the unmet desires express themselves in unhealthy ways, causing Eric to act out in moments of emotional vulnerability and make bad decisions. On one occasion, when Eric was at a particularly low point, he sought the company of some unsavoury individuals, and indulged in certain harmful substances along the way. He texted me to confess what he had done and also that he was feeling physically ill because of the substances he had abused. Knowing he needed urgent help and counsel, I rushed over to his home where he was resting and spent an extended period of time speaking and praying with him. He had been unable to confess what he had done to anyone else up until that point and I believe I was the first person to come to his aid. By God's grace, I'm glad to say that he always eventually turns back to God. Surely this is testament to how deeply-rooted his love for the Lord is, and that God has affirmed Eric on multiple occasions that His reward is greater.

Walking with Eric on this journey has made me realize how important it is for people with SSA to know that they are not only cherished by their church and Christian communities, but that they are not "less-than" simply because they are unable to (naturally) pursue a straight relationship. They still have a vital and important part to play in church, even if they choose to remain single for the rest of their lives. They need not be shunned or shut out of the church body simply because of their sexual orientation.

Seeing Eric choose God, *every single day*, over his natural inclinations and desires to have a relationship with another man reminds me that this is a lifelong battle that he will have to deal with. If God never takes his inclinations away,

Eric will have to fight this battle every day in order to stay pure and remain faithful to God. For Eric, choosing God really requires tremendous sacrifice and dying to self, on a scale that straight persons will never be able to understand.

Every day, he has to decide if he loves God more than his desire to settle down with a man that he might be in love with. Being able to get married and start a family with a person of the opposite gender whom we love—something that we straight people take for granted—is not an easy or readily available option for Eric. Eric loves children very much, so I can't imagine the pain he must feel knowing that he might never have his own biological children, simply because he might never get married.

Walking with Eric has also opened my eyes to see how the church needs to step in and take that place of the family that every same-sex attracted individual longs to have but may never have. Eric has a wonderful relationship with his godchildren and their parents—he loves his godchildren like they are his own and he is incredibly involved in their growing-up process, but only because his godchildren's parents have opened up their hearts to Eric and allowed him that kind of access into their kids' lives. Through having such a big hand in raising and taking care of his godchildren, Eric is fulfilling the role of a parent that he might not have if his friends were more concerned with "protecting" their kids from his influence instead of seeing what wonderful wholeness the presence of the children would bring to his life.

In his local church community as well, Eric is incredibly busy and fulfilled serving actively in various ministries. His dramatic skills and talent are recognized by the church leadership and he is allowed to flourish using his gifts for God there. He has also been able to disclose his sexual orientation to some of his church leaders and it has given him more freedom in relating to the leadership where it really matters. I have personally witnessed how Eric's local church community loves and cares for him on many levels, rallying around him and his family during the incredibly difficult time when his mother passed away, and always taking time to have meals with him, surprising him with presents (his love language is giving and receiving gifts!) and being willing helpers and participants whenever he directs church drama productions. I am deeply encouraged when I see how full his life in the Body of Christ is, particularly with his god-family and his local church, and can attest that it is definitely the fact that fellow believers have stepped in to surround and fill the many areas of his life, that he is better able, strengthened and more motivated to choose God on a daily basis, because he sees the reward.

As his sister-in-Christ and his co-worker, I have also pledged myself to be readily available to Eric for counsel, prayer and encouragement, particularly in the area of living out our faith in our industry. We both want to make a mark in the scene, but we want to do it in a way that honours God, and we have drawn great strength from doing this side by side. Our work environment can oftentimes be hostile towards us as believers, and I don't want him to be alone in defending our faith to our liberal colleagues.

In his church family, Eric sees that he is a vital part of the community—that he belongs and he has a home there. Eric sees a glimpse of heaven. He gets a preview of how rich and loving his eternity with Jesus will be, and it gives him hope and strength to not give up this fight. To choose God, *every single day*, and to be affirmed by the promises in 1 Peter 5:10 (ESV)—"...after you have suffered a little while, the God of all grace, who has called you to His eternal glory in Christ, will Himself restore, confirm, strengthen, and establish you."

I am convinced that if Christian individuals with SSA do not have the kind of support that Eric has, it will be a lot harder for them to stay faithful and a lot easier for them to turn away and seek community-life elsewhere, namely in circles where living a flagrant homosexual lifestyle is celebrated.

Linda Tan

* Read Eric's story on page 40.

FREED TO LOVE

It had been five years since Joe* told us he was gay. We were on a road trip with our friends and this was the first time he brought his partner along.

This trip was a first for many things—Joe's partner meeting us, us traveling with Joe and a partner, and Joe asking me point blank what I thought of his partner. I had met his previous partners, but those were usually just over a meal and quite once off.

This time though, we both sensed that Ben* was different. He was warm, loved God and people, actively served in church, and had a similar circle of friends and passions as I. We got along instantly, and Joe knew this would happen. He saw a future with Ben early in their relationship. He wanted to know if I saw the same thing for them, but Joe also knew my stand on homosexuality.

Joe and I had had chats about what we both knew the Bible says about homosexuality, but our conversations also included why and how he had decided to leave church, to leave positions of leadership he had held there, and to love as he felt most intuitively.

I would listen, aching inside, but mostly keep quiet because I knew that *he knew* what was right and wrong. He had earnestly tried to "rid himself" of his same-sex attraction (SSA) in all the ways he was told would help, but nothing worked. He finally decided after some years that he was done being made to feel guilty and judged. He felt he had to choose between staying in church and hiding his SSA, or leaving church to freely follow his desires. Since I did not know what else to do, I tended to say and do little for fear of pushing him away like others in the church had. So when Joe asked me a few days into our road trip what I thought of Ben, I felt like a deer caught in headlights. I felt the need to speak the truth but was there a way of saying it lovingly? Finally, I said, "You know where I stand on this. And I wish I could say I've never been happier for you because I *really* like Ben and I know you do too, but you know I can't".

In the years that followed, our group of friends, now including Ben, continued to travel, hang out together, and celebrate milestones in each other's lives. Yet, while most of us are Christians, we hardly, if ever, spoke about Joe and Ben with Joe or Ben. Not talking about the elephant in the room sure seemed like the safer option, to me at least.

Yet ever so often, I would feel guilty for not speaking up about their relationship and wondered if, by my silence, I was condoning it. Was I compromising what I believed by not talking them out of their relationship or even by keeping them close as friends? What was I supposed to pray for? That they would break up? Should I pray that God would use me as an instrument in that process? To assuage these feelings of guilt, I would try to sneak in a line or two about God and what He was doing in my life or ask about how Ben was doing in church in my effort to "keep God in the picture".

Needless to say, much of my effort was driven by guilt and curtailed by fear. Little did I realize that I was living under the law, which tells me what is right and wrong, but which offers no power to choose rightly. I was relating to Joe and Ben out of my own efforts to please God and keep them close, but was achieving neither.

> "Is it hard for Joe to relate to you now that you're in full-time ministry?"

Fast forward to a few months ago when Janice, another of Joe's close friends, sent me a text out of the blue with the above question. As I crafted my reply to her, it hit me that we had actually become much closer *despite* me being in full-time ministry. This amazed me because I had started off with the same worry as Janice that our relationship would go south. But God was about to show me another way forward. It would involve stepping back from trying to "force fit Jesus" into our conversations in my attempts to fix my friends and have them know Him. Even more significantly, He was going to bring me to a place where I could no longer rely on my own efforts to live for Him.

This shift happened not as I became savvier at slipping biblical truths into our conversation. Instead, it happened as God "turned the tables on me" and began to show me my own sin and brokenness that I had been blind to. And it happened when I least expected it to—right as I entered full-time ministry.

Instead of gearing up to be able to do more for the Lord, He began to show me little by little, yet more and more each time, how sinful I was and how little I understood of my need for His grace. As He unveiled areas of my life that were previously untouched or had gone unquestioned, I felt exposed and ashamed. I saw how my well-established coping mechanisms and strengths had hardened my heart and become hindrances to me turning to God. As I realized how much I needed His saving me from myself, He made known in even greater measure how pleased and ready He was to do just that.

I found myself grasping to know this God anew and wondering how I could have missed out on all this in my past years. I knew so little of His mercy, grace, and patience. I knew so little of what it meant to struggle honestly without falling back on religious platitudes to ease my discomfort or conscience. I finally felt free to wrestle with things like, "Why didn't You fix all this before I entered full-time ministry? Actually, why did You even call me into full-time ministry since You know perfectly how messed up I am?!" And as the Lord unravelled me and showed me how He saw me, I found myself processing and marvelling about many of these things with Joe and Ben. They were the ones who somehow knew when and how to be there for me, even when I did not know how to ask. They made me feel safe. They held no expectations I felt others in church had of me to have it all together. They listened, stuck close as I processed these raw and messy emotions, loved me well, and gave me all the time and space I needed to struggle and start afresh in many ways.

> I found myself grasping to know this God anew and wondering how I could have missed out on all this in my past years.

Through this very long season, Joe and Ben became some of my closest friends as I relearnt who I was, whose I was, who Jesus was to me, and who He is to them too. With all this being figured out as we talked and spent hours together, Jesus ended up being in every conversation we had without me having to intentionally try. Still, though, I was blind to how God was using them in my own journey of growth. Through them, imperfect as they were, I experienced so much of Jesus' deep love for me, though they were the very ones I once felt responsible to show His love to. They were the very instruments and means of the Lord's goodness and grace to me in my times of need.

Only after repeated instances of them loving and caring for me did it click that God was using them to change my view of Him—He doesn't require us to be sinless or "good enough" before He can use us in life or ministry. Quite the opposite, despite our sin and brokenness, He is *for* us. *He* will accomplish what we cannot do on our own as we surrender to Him. And He will help us surrender because He knows how hard it is and that we cannot do it on our own. As I learnt these truths for myself, I began to believe they are true for Joe and Ben too. I finally began to feel free to enjoy them as friends without the nagging feeling that it was my role to somehow "fix" them or try to convict them that their relationship was wrong.

God, who sees them for more than their gay relationship, is committed to turning their affections to Him, satisfying their desires perfectly as only He can and in His own ways and time. I can rest in His promise that "He who began a good work in you will bring it to completion at the day of Jesus Christ" and make it my prayer that their "love may abound more and more, with knowledge and all discernment, so that (they) may approve what is excellent, and so be pure and blameless for the day of Christ, filled with the fruit of righteousness that comes through Jesus Christ, to the glory and praise of God" (Philippians 1:6, 9–11).

After years of fearing that I would jeopardize our friendship if I spoke about the truth and light I claim to believe and live by, the Spirit of God revealed to me that *I* was the one "who loved the darkness rather than the light" and that *my* "works were evil" (John 3:19). Since "evil" refers to anything that flows from unbelief and is done apart from faith in Christ, I finally saw my fear for what it was. It stemmed from my unbelief that Jesus' love is an infinitely better love than what they share and can satisfy completely. It stemmed from my unbelief that the life Jesus promises all who call on His name is infinitely better than one we try to create and maintain for ourselves.

This revelation was not one of condemnation but an invitation to trust Him more—that He knows how important this friendship is to me, that He knows and loves and cares for Joe and Ben more than I ever can or will, and that His grace and mercy are far more abundant than I believe. As the Lord slowly kneads these truths into my heart, I am freed to relate in greater truth, both to Joe and Ben, and to Him. I am freed to love and reflect His heart better as I learn it for myself in the way He loves me. I am freed to enjoy the friendships He has given me. What freedom comes from being in the love of Christ and relating out of that love! What confidence I can have in Jesus and all that He will do for the glory and praise of God!

Eunice Lin

LOVING MY SAME-SEX ATTRACTED FRIENDS

I met David* and Sam* when I was in high school. With David, I immediately bonded over our mutual dislike of hypocrisy and perpetual desire to change the world. We were comfortable freethinkers and supportive of the freedom to love any way you wanted.

Sam, on the other hand, became a close friend of mine because of his attraction toward David. In fact, it was Sam who first came out to me as he was frustrated by David's lack of response to his advances. He wanted to know more from me about what David was thinking as he saw that I was close to David.

When this happened, I was excited but felt I needed to give David the space to make the decision. When David broke the news to me that he was in a relationship with another man—Sam—I could not have been more pleased and happy for him.

At around the same time, I also came to realize that my attraction towards both women and men was not something that everybody experienced. I had always assumed everybody experienced sexual attraction to both genders, but for biological reasons it was just practical to publicly discuss and marry one gender. I never knew this was considered "different" or "abnormal". So, realising that we were different—and on the cusp of something unknown, unexplored, and dangerous—it was an exciting time for us three to be able to journey this together as friends.

But things did not work out according to my plans. I was in a relationship with a guy at the time but had asked for a break as I was not sure where the relationship was going. During the break, I met and was deeply attracted to a girl. Eventually, I decided to continue the relationship with my ex-boyfriend. That didn't last long.

In my second year of university, I went for a volunteering trip in Kenya, Africa. There, I lived with a family and saw the faith of people who believed fervently in a God even though their circumstances were so dire. It made me see that true joy and happiness cannot be found anywhere else—not in self acceptance or success—but in believing in something greater. Watching the night sky full of stars connected me with this presence I always knew was in my life. Peaceful, patient, warm, loving. It was also around that time that I had a phone conversation with my ex-boy-friend who was really upset that I wasn't around for his matriculation. This was in such contrast to a phone call I made to my parents who were concerned and relieved that I had called. It showed me what true love looked like and showed me how little I knew of it.

So, when I got back to the UK to continue my studies, I had this desire to explore Christianity again because I remembered how the cross—Jesus dying for us—had always moved me. And it was also this gentle prompting in my heart ... a voice that said I had to choose. So I chose the voice, and then, loud and clear, while I was crying from the pain of it, the voice said "Go back to church". It was a soft, gentle beckoning to come find out for myself what Love really is. I said yes to God by leaving my ex-boyfriend, who was adamant that I should not explore Christianity as that would lead to us breaking up; he was right. And I began to understand over time that truth, objective truth, is found only in the Creator, and that Love has a name. It was a painful yes that cost me everything I knew. Yet, in exchange, God finally had my attention and the space to show me what it meant when Jesus said: "... whoever loses their life for my sake will find it." (Matthew 10:39)

The test of my faith in God and His ability to provide for and lead me came when Sam confronted me about my faith. This was about a couple of months into discovering who God is. I was aware of the inconsistency—we had agreed to explore our sexuality together just a year earlier and yet now I was thoroughly convinced that Christ is the answer.

Sam, having grown up in a Christian household, probably knew the Bible better than I did. He had a loving family, solid upbringing in church, was loving and lovable, and yet struggled with his identity as a son of God because of the unique nature of the temptation he was facing. Nobody knew, and even when they did, they did not know what to say to him. His parents were disappointed but chose to love and embrace him.

When he asked whether I would vote to repeal 377A,[1] I felt

---

1   Section 377A ("Outrages on decency") of the Penal Code of Singapore states: any male person who, in public or private, commits, or abets the commission of, or procures or attempts to procure the commission by any male person of, any act of gross indecency with another male person, shall be punished with imprisonment for a term who may extend to 2 years.

sad and afraid. Sad, because I could tell that he was challenging me out of hurt, and afraid because I was scared of losing my friendship with him if I spoke the truth. I wanted him to know that he was not any different, any less valued, any less loved, yet at the same time, I could not conceal the truth because the truth would set us both free. So I said no, I would not vote to repeal it, because I believed that the law should be aligned to biblical values. He bristled at my response. And in that moment, somehow, God gave me the words and the heart to say, "Sam, if anybody ever comes to you threatening you, hurting you, or even wanting to kill you for this, I would stand between you and that person and defend you because I love you, I recognize your free will to choose how you want to live and there is no place for discrimination in the Bible." By the grace of God, Sam's heart softened and he gave me a deep hug, which was really rare between us, and we parted ways with a solid assurance of love and where we stood with each other.

It is still tense at times, when we talk about Jesus. He thinks that I am inconsistent in my beliefs, especially when it comes to the age-old argument of why God is against same-sex relationships if He is so good. There's nothing wrong, we are not hurting anybody, and you are still standing for us and you are our friend, he would argue. I did not quite know how to explain that anything that goes against God's design has a negative consequence eventually. This was based on faith in His Word. And I am keenly aware that Christians are not always shining examples of Christ, which makes it hard to show the difference when one trusts in God's design. I am far from a shining example myself, and I have come to realize that it will take God to glorify Himself through me and to convict and convince them. In the meantime, I can only rely on God and seek Him to find comfort in His presence and company.

With David, breaking the news that I had become a Christian was much easier, because we had always accepted the fact that we are different, will always be different, and that we will want to continue being there for each other regardless of our choices. What was painful and difficult for me was when David asked what I thought about homosexuality specifically—not because I thought it was difficult to convey the truth—but because I was afraid that he would think that my love for him had somehow changed because of what the Bible says about homosexuality.

Before God, I had a choice to make. Do I trust Him to lead me to speak the truth in love? Do I trust that the truth is the word of God and will set us free? I struggled, He won. God made a way in a conversation for me to share how much He had changed my life. I explained to David how being a Christian means believing in the entire Bible, but that the Bible also says that I am not any better than he is, or any worse. I'm saved and am living every day free only by the grace of God. He paused, held it in, accepted it, and embraced me. In that moment, I knew God had spoken and moved, and that we would be friends and walk this together, because God is love, and love never fails.

Today, David and Sam are still close friends of mine. We still share about our lives and agree to disagree. Though it is hard at times, God keeps me close to Him. I am still working out certain things with God—for example, is it acceptable for me to attend their wedding if they ever get married? Is it wrong for me to exclaim in delight and offer to sing at their wedding because they have chosen this path despite knowing the truth? Is it okay that I don't have a sorrowful spirit about it as I have done my part to speak the truth? There are moments that I wonder if this is hindering me from the full experience of carrying my cross, which includes denying my own desire for friendship. I do not know, but I trust that Jesus does and He will continue to lead me. Maybe someday that will mean stepping away from these friendships, but until the conviction and confirmation comes, I will continue to walk in the conviction that salt needs to be in contact with the world to prevent decay. Light needs to be unveiled in dark places so that people will know where to come home to.

Sometimes, walking with people with SSA is just like walking with any other person. When we look to Christ to lead and ask for His eyes to see them, we soon realize that we are all the same in our sinfulness before God. Broken, wretched, deeply in need of the blood of Christ. We all need to wait for His timing, obey His leading, and respond to Him in relationship so that others may know what that looks like. It is really that simple, and it will only be by the word of God and the Holy Spirit's leading that we can walk this out day by day. The verses below sum it all up.

> *"Jesus replied: 'Love the Lord your God with all your heart and with all your soul and with all your mind.' This is the first and greatest commandment. And the second is like it: 'Love your neighbor as yourself.' All the Law and the Prophets hang on these two commandments."* (Matthew 22:37–40 NIV)

Lenda Lee

BEING A FRIEND

I was 17 when I first started leading a cell group of 13-year-olds. Out of all the youth in the cell, Sara* was probably the most outspoken. She was always bubbly and happy and she made cell a fun place to be. As time passed, however, she became more and more reserved. I started to notice marks on her arms, which were indicative of where she had self-harmed with a pen-knife or a pair of scissors. Each time I tried to talk to her about how she was doing, she wouldn't share much with me. Admittedly, I wasn't doing so well myself and hadn't taken the time to cultivate the sense of trust that would have helped her feel safe sharing more vulnerably.

If memory serves, Sara and I both stopped going to church around the same time, albeit for different reasons. I took a break from leading the cell, telling my youth that it was because I needed to deal with my struggles with anxiety. In reality, I was disillusioned with Christianity and simply wanted to be done with it. I was also tired of leading the cell group week after week, as I was increasingly feeling that it was both burdensome as well as futile. I didn't believe the hope I told my youth about and they didn't seem to want to be at cell either. What was the point?

In the two years that followed, I went on my own journey of running away from Christianity, to realizing life was hopeless without God, to discovering more of who God was and the depth of His love for me. Having experienced the love of God for myself, I returned to church and cell-leading with a newfound joy and passion. For the first time, cell-leading was both meaningful and deeply important to me. I was acutely aware, however, of the fact that some of the youth who used to attend cell regularly had stopped coming altogether. I also struggled with feelings of guilt because I believed that it was largely my fault that they had stopped coming. Thus, I took on the mission of trying to get all the missing youth to return to cell—Sara being one of them. Initially, Sara didn't seem very interested. She would give non-committal replies to my text messages, and when asked about how she was doing, wouldn't share more than two sentences, if at all. After months of these short conversations over text, Sara dropped me a message one day asking if we could meet for lunch.

I'm not sure what I was expecting, but I certainly did not expect the honesty and vulnerability with which Sara shared about her life when we did meet. She talked about how she struggled with feelings of despair and a deep sense of self-hatred. She shared about how she'd been trying to stop self-harming, only to fail time and time again. These were difficult things for her to talk about, but I know that the hardest thing for her to admit was that at the heart of this struggle was the fact that she was same-sex attracted. It didn't come as a total surprise to me that Sara struggled with same-sex attraction (SSA); I think some part of me already knew. The only thing I remember saying to her was that I loved her and that this didn't change the way I saw her and valued her. And yet, I could see it in her eyes that even as she was nodding in acknowledgement, she didn't fully believe me.

On the way home that day, I had many questions for God. The most pressing question however, was, "What should I do about this?" On hindsight, I think what I was really asking God was, "How do I help to fix her?"

We continued to meet for lunch regularly, but I struggled with what to say much of the time. Do I quote scripture? Do I recommend a book to her to read? I was 19 at the time, still a kid myself, and there was no manual for what to do in this situation.

One day, as I was talking to God about how helpless I felt, I sensed God telling me not to focus on the fact that Sara struggled with SSA, as I had been doing thus far. God was telling me that Sara was so much more than her SSA and that I needed to help her remember that this struggle didn't define who she was. In the following months, I began to ask more about her other interests. As she shared her passions and her dreams, it's like the heaviness lifted and Sara came alive. In these conversations, I started to catch glimpses of the Sara I knew at 13.

My Journey with Bella

Apart from Sara, there was another girl in the cell who had stopped coming for a good amount of time. Unlike Sara, Bella* had always been quiet and had struggled to fit in with the rest of the cell since the beginning. I would message her too, encouraging her to come back to church and cell. But like Sara, she didn't seem interested at first.

At the close of 2016, I got a text message from one of my co-cell leaders that Bella had gone to church that day and had been sobbing uncontrollably at the entrance of the service hall. He said that she didn't say much, but that they had attended service together after she had calmed down. That night, after I had dropped her a text message to ask if she was okay, Bella asked to meet. Much like my initial meeting with Sara, Bella was surprisingly honest. She shared about how she struggled with self-rejection, and a deep sense of inadequacy.

Bella had tried, on multiple occasions, to come back to church. Each time, she was so afraid that she would stand outside the church gates for long periods of time debating with herself about whether to walk in or not. The day my co-cell leader saw her sobbing in church was, in fact, the first time in over a year that she'd managed to muster up the courage to actually walk into church. As she poured her heart out, both of us wept over how much pain she was feeling. Two weeks later, Bella, who was 16 at this point, returned to cell. We all told her how incredibly happy we were to have her back. I don't think I will ever forget the smile that spread across her face.

A few months after Bella started coming regularly for church and cell, she came to me crying before the start of service. We found a quiet spot to sit and talk and I waited for her to feel ready enough to share what was on her heart. She squeezed her hands together, and repeatedly said she didn't know how to say the words she needed to say. I told her it was okay and to take all the time she needed. Finally, Bella said between sobs, "I...I think I'm not exactly straight. I sometimes feel like I like girls and I don't know why. Nobody knows this. My family doesn't know this. They would never see me the same way. I don't know what to do." It was clear to me, at this point, that this was a big part of why Bella had been struggling with self-rejection. I prayed with her and told her that as disgusted as she felt with herself, God looked upon her with gentleness and compassion.

"You are beautiful to Him. You are His precious daughter," I wept as we prayed. I remember feeling deeply broken and anguished. In that moment, it wasn't about finding the right words to say or the right verse to quote to solve the problem. To sit with Bella and to share her pain was all that was needed. She had felt intensely alone in this struggle thus far, so to simply be there with her in this area of pain was what was most pertinent then.

Today, both Sara and Bella still struggle with SSA and it remains a key source of confusion and struggle in both of their lives. In spite of this, I have learned to see that they are so much more than this particular struggle and it does not define who they are. I have experienced many moments of joy and laughter in the time spent walking with each of them and they are precious sisters to me. Through being their cell leader, I have learned a great deal about brokenness, courage, and the love of God. Most of all, I have learned that at the heart of it, what is required of me is to simply be their friend.

Amanda Foo

A SPACE IN THE GARDEN

It all started six years ago when I found out that a close church friend of mine, whom I had known for many years, was gay. That revelation broke my heart because I realized that even though we had been friends for so many years, he did not feel comfortable enough to tell me. I found out from someone else. Questions came to me. Why couldn't he tell me? Since when was he gay? Oh, how he must have struggled all these years trying to hide it!

Because this topic hit so close to home, I felt the impetus to find out more about it. I started asking my gay friends about their sexuality. When did you know you were gay? Did you ever like someone of the opposite sex? Do you think you can change?

At about the same time, Christopher Yuan's testimony[1] on YouTube was circulating online and I was deeply impacted as I watched it. Hearing from my gay friends, watching Christopher Yuan's video testimony, and reading his book *Out of A Far Country*, gave me a deeper insight into the psyche of gay people, their struggles, and what God desires for them.

---

1   Christopher Yuan is an American author and is currently teaching the Bible at Moody Bible Institute. Together with his mother, he co-authored the book *Out of a Far Country: A Gay Son's Journey to God, A Broken Mother's Search for Hope.*

I realized that many Christians do not have a clear understanding about homosexuality, and hence the first important step we need to make is to gain a deeper understanding of what it means to be gay, and then how a gay person might perceive the words and actions of the Christian community. If not, we may make unhelpful judgements or comments which could hurt the gay community. There were many things I learnt, but I will share three here. First, most gay people (and I only speak for males as those were the ones I interacted with) do not "choose" to be gay. Their same-sex attraction (SSA) is something natural to them, just as our opposite-sex attraction is for us heterosexuals. One poignant comment my gay friend made which really struck me was, "Why would I choose to be gay? It's so hard!" This explains why many gay people would have tried straight relationships, in their desperate attempt to prove to themselves they are not gay.

Second, the Christian approach towards gay people should not be about "converting them" to becoming straight. I have learnt from Christopher Yuan that it is about pursuing holy sexuality, and that applies to all of us, whether we are same-sex attracted or straight, single or married. It is about celibacy in singleness and fidelity in marriage. So, since a gay person is not biblically permitted to be in a relationship with someone of the same sex, then they are called to celibacy, just as any straight single person is.

Third, I've learnt that it is not helpful to generalize the gay community; gay people are as different one to another, as straight people are. Just as we would not say that all straight people have multiple relationships or like to club or are creatively-inclined, so too we cannot make the same assumption or generalization of a gay person.

My Ministry

I soon found myself going with a group of gay people to church on weekends, as they were interested in settling into a church. However, that proved to be more difficult than expected. When one of them opened up about his sexual orientation (something many gay people find difficult to do) to church leaders at the end of a membership interview, he was met with blank responses. Neither he, nor any of the rest were invited to join a cell, and instead were told that they had to repent before they would be accepted as members. Unable to be part of the church community, they continued to attend services on the weekends, but I wondered if they felt rejected by the church. I felt strongly that what my friends needed was to grow in their understanding of the Word of God, and to grow as believers. If they did not know God's Word, how would they know who God really is and how He wants them to live? Because they had difficulty assimilating into a church, I felt God nudging me to start a Bible study group for them, so that we could study the Word together.

For me, shepherding a group of same-sex attracted Christian males in Bible study was totally out of my realm of contemplation and comfort, and I felt deeply unqualified to do so, as a heterosexual female. However, I knew that I had the Lord as my guide. I did not choose this ministry, but God gave it to me so that I would learn to rely on Him alone and not on my own abilities.

A Motley and Warm Fellowship

The group of us would gather every week to study the Word of God. Although we started with a handful of same-sex attracted Christians, God soon added to our group a variety of new members from diverse backgrounds. We had people struggling with divorce, those battling cancer, those from dysfunctional families, singles, and so on. I often wondered why our group was not the "usual" Christian group, but I believe God brought us all together for a reason. I encouraged authentic sharing from group members from the beginning. Wonderfully, we became candid about sharing our struggles, joys, prayer requests, and views about the passages we were studying—without fear of judgement. And so, that built deep bonds among the members, and our fellowship was warm, close, and often filled with laughter. We were not afraid to challenge each other's viewpoints or challenge each other to change. There was never a boring moment!

Real Struggles, Real Outcomes

One of the struggles I had as a group leader was how much I should bring up the topic of homosexuality and what the Bible taught about it. On the one hand, I wondered if it was my "duty" to bring it up and to challenge members in this area. Yet on the other hand, I felt that I had to also be a friend and to show acceptance, and it wouldn't be nice to keep bringing the topic up. After all, we are all sinners and fallen. We are all struggling with sin. Who would like it if their cell leader kept singling out the sin they were struggling with? How would that make them feel? So in the end, I erred on the side of caution, and was circumspect about bringing it up.

Instead, I focused on building friendships first so they knew that, first and foremost, I was their friend. I wanted to show them love, and that I genuinely cared. This way, if God should give me the opportunity to speak about SSA, they would know I am coming from a place of care, not judgement. And God definitely did give me opportunities to speak to them, on a one-to-one basis. I think all the gay people in my group knew where I stood on this matter. And sometimes, I felt that that was enough.

We met as a group for a few years, and grew to really love and care for each other. One of the gay members said that he could be open about his sexuality in our group, but felt he couldn't be the same way in his own church cell group. If you ask me today if I think they have grown in their knowledge of the Word and their love of God, I would say yes. Do I see significant changes in their relationships (for instance, have they decided to give up their partners and choose celibacy)? Maybe not. Yes, I do feel guilty some-times, and wonder if I have done enough to shed light on the topic of homosexuality and to encourage members to live holy lives in this area. I wonder if I've failed as their Bible study leader when I don't see the changes.

But I cling on to a personal message which Christopher Yuan sent me, when I wrote to him early on in this ministry to ask for advice in this area. What he said encourages me till today. He said, "Thank you for reaching out to your (gay) friend. Our goal is not to 'fix' your friend because only God can change a person." Isn't this amazing? We often go around trying to "fix" people, and for some reason, we focus so much on the gay Christian. But ultimately, only God can convict a person about change, and change the person—and that includes us! So what makes us think that we can change a gay person? Only the Almighty God can do that, in His own gracious way and time.

A Space in the Garden
I was reluctant to write this story at first because I felt that I didn't have much to show for my journey with these

friends; no grand testimony to speak of. However, a friend told me that that was not true, and shared that what mattered was that I gave my gay friends a place where they could feel accepted and could engage on Christian issues. Most of them don't even feel accepted in church. The job of changing them is God's. The job of showing acceptance is the Christian leaders'.

I gave them a place to sit and stand—literally and figuratively. It's like a gardener giving them a space in the garden, and some soil. Maybe they won't grow, maybe they will. But if one doesn't even get a space in the garden, where does one get one's food? If one doesn't even have soil, how will someone else apply the fertilizer? They were accepted and they had the Word and prayer filling their hearts. And these are the bits that add up. It's the amount of kindness you receive that allows you to give the kindness back. Here they found friendship, acceptance, and love, and that is how they can find and know God. As for the change? I can only trust God to bring it about in His own time and way, because He loves them far more than I do or can ever imagine.

My desire for the Christian community is that it will develop a better understanding of what it means to have SSA, will reach out to people with SSA, and will show them love and acceptance. I pray that we will give them space in the garden—the Christian community—so that God the Gardener can work in their lives. If they don't feel welcomed by Christians and the Church, they will turn to the world for acceptance. We have all sinned and fallen short of the glory of God. We are not an elite club, so let's not single out people with SSA to meet higher standards. We are all subject to the same standards, which Christ has paid the price for, and we all need the same transforming power and love of God.

Carrie Ty

EQUALLY YOKED

I studied at a Methodist secondary school where discussions on same-sex attraction (SSA) were limited and taboo. Teachers would sweep the topic under the rug, sometimes proclaiming that being LGBTQ is merely a passing phase. My schoolmates and I would thus speculate on what a homosexual person was like. Of course, there were students among us whom we suspected of being homosexual, but because of the hostile attitudes towards the topic, they would stay in the closet and our suspicions were never confirmed.

I went on to read Film Studies at a local polytechnic, and it was there that I had more exposure to the LGBTQ community, as the faculty had an international mix and the industry was a lot more liberal. It was also then that I started to interact with same-sex attracted friends and lecturers.

Being a Christian, I could never have imagined myself eventually marrying a same-sex attracted individual. In my mind, I had expected my adult life to be more run-of-the-mill than the way it turned out to be.

Out of the Frying Pan...and into the Oven
To cut a long story short, I became an intern at a life-development company at the age of 26 (after recovering from a road traffic accident that had left me severely injured). Unbeknownst to me, I had unwittingly entered an

environment which espoused values that were friendly to the LGBTQ community.

It was there that I met my future wife, Val. Just like Princess Leia and Han Solo in *Star Wars*, Val and I came from two very different worlds. I was instantly attracted to her (I found out on hindsight that she did not feel the same way towards me until just before we started dating). After probing around, I found out that Val was same-sex attracted—but it did not dampen my interest in her. Instead, I decided to play the waiting game, to wait for the right opportunity to tell her how I felt about her.

At the time, Val had a girlfriend and they appeared to be happy together. However, as I got to know Val better, I found out that she was deeply unhappy with her partner who was abusive and controlling. The cracks in their relationship soon became apparent as they often fought over trivial matters. To make things even more complicated, I found out that her partner was jealous about my accomplishments as well as my friendship with Val. This caused tension among the three of us.

By this time, I had known Val well enough to know that although her lifestyle choices were unholy, she was not a malicious and evil person at heart. I was convinced that I would be a better romantic fit for her than her partner even though I knew that approaching a same-sex attracted person for a legitimate and lasting relationship was not only high risk, but out of left field. All I could think of then was that if she were to receive Christ, God would be able to use her mightily. You see, Val is extremely good with people, and it was not difficult to see that she would make a great ministry leader.

That thought, along with what I believed to be God's prompting, led me to take the step to express my feelings for her. However, Val rejected me, stating that she was committed to her job and that she needed to focus on it. For some inexplicable reason, I took the rejection rather well.

Crossing the Chasm that Felt like a Ditch

Whether it was tenacity or stubbornness, I held on to the hope that Val would reconsider, and the opportunity came when I met Val's mother a month later.

It was over a dinner at East Coast, and we had a good time together. After dropping off Val's mother at home, I decided to broach the topic again with Val, after she had returned from walking her mother back to the apartment. To my surprise, Val said yes, and ended her relationship with her girlfriend. Weeks later, I found out from Val that her mother had told her that I was a good match for her as they were walking to the apartment that night, and that prompted Val to accept me as a suitor.

My relationship with Val was not without challenges. There were people in my previous company who opposed our relationship (please read Val's story to find out more). Before Val became a Christian, my sensibilities were tested as we held completely different, sometimes even hostile, worldviews and values on family and friends. There was virtually no one, other than God, I could consult when there were obstacles in our relationship, and this made it a lot harder for me.

Also, I had to keep modifying my expectations as I ventured into this new terrain. For instance, some women worry about whether their male spouse is cheating on them with other females. But with Val, who is attracted to people of both genders, this meant she could be stumbled more easily than most people.

Marriage was a topic that we found virtually impossible to see eye to eye about. Val wanted to feel she belonged and was loved; I wanted to feel I belonged, was loved, and *was married*. Marriage in the biblical sense was something that Val had never thought of. By God's grace, I was given an even temperament and a boatload of patience. God also provided me help from my church's senior pastor and showed me the right thing to say to her at the right time to address her questions regarding the faith, evolution, gender roles, and the reliability and infallibility of the Bible.

At the same time, I had resolved in my heart not to marry her if she did not accept Christ, as I did not believe we could go the distance if we were unequally yoked. But finally, with the help of the Holy Spirit, I was able to speak emotionally simple and intellectually provable biblical truths to Val, which led her to be convinced of the truth of Jesus Christ.

Val eventually accepted Christ in 2015, and we married in 2016.

God Did the Heavy Lifting

As we journeyed together in the following years, we eventually came to accept that our situation—a same-sex attracted woman married to a straight man—had few precedents. And it has certainly been a lonely journey. My personal take is that the church's lack of exposure to

LGBTQ persons and the perception it gives to the outsider about its opposition to alternative lifestyles make it hard for individuals like Val to feel welcomed. That, in fact, was the reason why Val shunned Christians initially.

And because of that, I often get asked, "What did you do to her?" Yet, I did not do much. God did most of the heavy lifting. God in His wonderful mercy presented us with each other at the most perfect timing. I just showed up at the right place at the right time to do my part in the right way.

Evans Wu

A MOTHER'S JOURNEY

When my daughter Val was just two, her father and I divorced. Day-to-day care of Val was given to her father with my consent, as I did not think that I could juggle a job and give her the best care possible. I also did not want her to be plucked away from a familiar environment. Val's father eventually married the woman who had broken up our marriage.

At the age of four, Val could not read or write, despite being in pre-kindergarten. Her father agreed to let me spend weeknights with Val in their home to teach her. So every evening, I would travel there, have dinner prepared by their helper and just spend time with Val. This arrangement could work because I had already forgiven Val's father and his wife by this time, and they were not home most nights. I was thankful to be able to be with Val and explained to her from an early age that all was well and the only difference was that I did not live in the same house as her. Before I left every evening, I would tuck her into bed. I was very involved in Val's life from kindergarten all the way through secondary school. When Val was 10, her father took up a job overseas and only came home to visit every three months. By this time, I had also learnt that Val's stepmother was verbally and mentally abusive to Val whenever she lost at gambling, which was often.

Val went to an all-girls secondary school. One day, when Val was in Secondary 2, I received a phone call at work from Val's helper, whom I had grown very close to. She told me that a girl, who was dressed like a boy, was visiting Val every day after school and they were behaving intimately. When I saw Val that evening, I told her that she should stop seeing this girl as it was against the norm and that it was not acceptable for two girls to be dating each other. But their "relationship" continued until one day when they had a big fight. The girl became violent and broke Val's main door, and the police had to be called. Later, I counselled Val and thought that this was just a one-off incident and that her same-sex attraction (SSA) phase was over.

All appeared to be well after this episode. I continued to be a supportive parent and participated in every school event, from parent-teacher meetings to concerts to annual school open-houses to the annual sports day. Val's grades improved significantly at the GCE 'O' level examinations and she went on to polytechnic. She even started dating boys.

In 2004, Val and her boyfriend left for university in Australia. They were planning on getting married and staying on in Australia after graduation.

I remarried in 2005 and Val would live with me whenever she came home during university breaks twice a year. Her boyfriend who was also back for the holidays visited us often. So I did not suspect at all that she still had SSA. She later revealed to me that she was dating boys just to please me and as a facade to hide her SSA from me.

In the meantime, her father and stepmother's marriage broke down and they soon divorced. But the verbal and mental abuse from her stepmother, the absence of her father, and my divorce from her father must have deeply hurt Val.

To my dismay, Val and her boyfriend broke up, and she returned to Singapore after her graduation. That was when I discovered that she was involved with a girl.

In 2009, she opened up to me about her SSA. To say that I was devastated was an understatement. My entire world came crashing down on me. I felt betrayed, deceived, and my heart ached. I scolded her, cajoled her, and told her that it was all wrong. I was a wreck, constantly crying and blaming myself for her SSA. I felt she had brought shame to our family and I even thought about disowning her. I phoned Val's father and told him about Val's sexual orientation, but to my surprise, he accepted it. This is not happening, it's just a nightmare that I would wake up from and everything would be fine, I kept telling myself. Val was aware of how upset I was and gave me a DVD on SSA to watch, in the hope that I would be able to understand what she was going through. I did not have the courage to watch it and got my husband to watch it instead. He was very supportive through it all and encouraged me to accept Val for what she was or end up losing her forever.

> I scolded her, cajoled her, and told her that it was all wrong. I was a wreck, constantly crying and blaming myself for her SSA.

To keep myself sane, I took my husband's advice to accept Val and also her girlfriend. I decided to tell my siblings and their families about Val's SSA and much to my surprise, they embraced Val and her new girlfriend. In fact, I became fond of this girl as well because she was pleasant and well-mannered.

Despite my acceptance of Val's SSA, I knew very well that SSA was against God's will. It was at this time that I turned back to God, our loving Father whom I had abandoned through the years. But now I went on my knees, asked God for forgiveness and prayed fervently for His divine intervention to stop Val's SSA.

My prayers went unanswered because Val went on to have another girlfriend, after her relationship (with the girl whom I liked) broke down. They became devoted to an LGBTQ community. I was extremely unhappy as this new girlfriend was very domineering and rude.

I did not give up hope. I prayed ceaselessly and trusted in God to work a miracle in Val's life. Val was admitted to hospital in July 2014 for a slipped disc. During her hospital stay, Evans, a friend whom she knew from her work, visited her. Evans and I struck up a conversation and I was impressed by him as he exuded confidence and was different from all of Val's friends whom I had met.

I saw him again at a music gig organized by Val, a day after she was discharged from the hospital. Not only was he charming, he was also a talented musician. I told Val that I knew that she would not date a guy, but I would be happy if I could see him again because I liked him. The following week I had the opportunity to meet him again, and I said to Val that this guy would make a nice boyfriend, if only she was interested.

A few days later, I returned to Canada where I have been residing for some years now. Naturally I began to worry again for Val and her well-being, as she was alone in Singapore with her new domineering girlfriend. Shortly after, Val told me that she and Evans[1] were dating. My immediate reaction to her was, "oh that's nice", but deep inside I thought she could be trying to please me again by telling me that she was dating a guy. I didn't press her again for further news about her new boyfriend for two reasons. If it were not true, I did not want to be disappointed again. But if it were indeed true, then it was a positive first step in my prayers being heard.

Val related to me later on that she encouraged Evans to go back to church, which he had not been to since he suffered an accident eight years ago. She had also fallen away from God and had not been to church since her early teens. It was at this first church attendance that Val heard Raphael Zhang, a guest speaker, address the issue of SSA. She told me that God finally answered her questions about homosexuality. She felt understood by God— that He had not made her this way and was not trying to turn her away but to call her back to Him. Val decided to be obedient to God's Word and began attending church regularly from then on because of how God had spoken to her through Raphael. One day, I received a call from her informing me that she and Evans were attending a marriage preparation course as they were planning to be married. Praise the Lord!

Val and Evans got married in 2016. God has showered His blessings on them. They welcomed their first-born son in

---

1   Please read Evans' and Val's stories for details.

November 2017. Val still struggles with SSA but practices obedience according to what God commands in the Bible and continues to seek Him. Val and Evans have been saved by the mercy and love of our Almighty God and are continuing in their walk with our Lord Jesus Christ. I thank and praise our Almighty God for His answer to my prayers in His own perfect timing.

Jez Lee

TRUSTING THE FATHER

A few years ago, my son confided in my wife and I that he was gay. Though we had suspected it for a while, we had refused to believe it then. Yet, my wife and I felt a great sense of relief when he came out into the open about his sexual orientation; I know he felt the same way too. Since then, our relationship with him has improved as he is now willing to confide in us about his struggles despite his opposing views about God and Christianity.

But the road leading up to it was a very difficult and painful one, due largely in part to my inexperience and insensitivity as a father.

My son is reserved by nature. He used to follow my wife and I to church as a child. I remember praying with him to receive Jesus as his Lord and Saviour. He would attend children's fellowship regularly. Little did I know that at that young age, he had already started struggling with feelings of attraction to boys. He had kept it to himself, confused and afraid to be called weird or abnormal.

Instead, we were preoccupied with wanting my son to achieve academic excellence in his studies. On hindsight, I realize that underlying our "good intentions" as parents for him to excel in order to have a good future, was the temptation to brag about our kid's achievements in the presence of friends and relatives. Unwittingly, we had neglected his emotional well-being.

I clearly remember the day my son came home happily to present his PSLE results to my wife and I, thinking that he had done well. I could not hide the disappointment on my face; I know he must have noticed the frown on my face as the joy on his face also disappeared. I have since repented and asked God to forgive me for being such a selfish and insensitive father back then.

My son went on to attend youth service in church. He came home after one youth camp to tell us how he had been touched by the Spirit and that he kept crying during the service. At school, however, he experienced bullying. During my son's teenage years, my relationship with him was also tumultuous. We had frequent fights as I was very critical of him. It was so bad that on one occasion, he took a kitchen knife and threatened me. Sunday mornings became very unpleasant when he started to refuse to join us for church and I realized I could not force him. I knew I needed to change. Instead of getting him to repent, I needed to repent myself—of my pride, selfishness, and anger.

Later in his secondary school years, my son stopped joining us for church and stopped attending the youth group altogether. He became hostile towards God and Christianity and started questioning the loving nature of God, asking questions such as, "why did God allow suffering and abortion?", and "why did he allow mankind to fall into sin?"

During his second year of junior college, he dropped out of school due to an incident where he felt he was unfairly disciplined. He became depressed and withdrawn. He had few friends and had frequent mood swings. He also switched to a vegetarian diet, became very picky over the food he ate, and reduced his food intake substantially, eating only one meal a day and sleeping most of the day. As a result, he lost much weight. It was very painful for us as parents to see him deteriorating not only mentally, but physically.

Concerned, my wife and I decided to consult a psychiatrist who prescribed him with anti-depressant drugs. However, he refused to take any medication. His mood swung depending on how his relationships with his friends fared. On several occasions, he became suicidal due to some relationship fallouts.

It was only after he told my wife and I that he was gay that he became more stable and better able to relate to the both of us. Thinking about how he had to hide his feelings for years and struggle to relate with his friends, I can now understand why he was in such a depressive state then.

Till today, I still wonder why my child has same-sex attraction (SSA). Was it due to my lack of parental care and protection? Or is this an inborn trait? The one thing I know for a fact though is that both SSA and non-SSA people are all the same, as we are all sinners loved by God. SSA is not a physical sickness. All sinners, regardless of whether or not they have SSA, need God's healing, deliverance, and restoration.

Finding support

After finding out about my son's SSA, my wife and I looked around for help. Despite being in my local church for many years, my wife and I felt spiritually dry and had no one to confide in, and pray along with us for our situation. We did not feel comfortable to share as the church had never openly mentioned its acceptance of SSA people. Neither was there any ministry to support parents with SSA children. Perhaps it is a taboo and sensitive topic. Perhaps they have no answer for it. So we decided to join another church to worship in anonymity.

In November 2015, we heard that Pastor Ben from Focus on the Family had initiated a support group for parents with SSA children. For the first time, we got to meet with other parents with SSA children who shared similar challenges. We were very encouraged and blessed.

As I recall our darkest moments and struggles, when we were at our wits' end, I remember how my wife and I went down on our knees before God to cry for help. For where else does our help come from but the Lord, the Maker of heaven and earth (Ps 121:1)? We clung on to God's word and His promises because He is our faithful God. His Holy Spirit sustains and strengthens us through His word. Each time we cry to Him desperately for help, we see His miraculous deliverance. For His way is always higher than our ways (Isa 55:9) and He "is able to do immeasurably more than all we ask or imagine" (Eph 3:20).

Today, my son is an adult. God has graciously protected and sustained him through the years. My son's condition is more stable now and our relationship has improved though he remains same-sex attracted and is still opposed to God. We are constantly praying for God to restore faith in him to acknowledge Jesus as his Lord and Saviour and God as his heavenly Father. I firmly believe that God's work in his life is not over; my son is still a "work in progress". I believe the ultimate answer to his healing and transformation is Jesus.

Till then, I choose to keep my faith to trust God that the day (be it in or after my lifetime) will come when my son will turn back to God and that his life will bring glory to God.

> As Jesus went along, He saw a man blind from birth. His disciples asked him, "Rabbi, who sinned, this man or his parents, that he was born blind?" Neither this man nor his parents sinned," said Jesus, "but this happened so that the works of God might be displayed in him." (John 9:1–3)

Aldrin Lee

A FATHER'S UNCONDITIONAL LOVE

I didn't have an earthly father who knew the Lord. My own father underwent the rigours of World War II and the Japanese Occupation. His life exposure moulded him to be a hard disciplinarian who showed his love by bringing back the bacon and using the cane for discipline. Having been brought up that way, I unwittingly took on my father's ways in the upbringing of my own children, seeing my role mainly as providing for my sons to enable them to succeed materially, neglecting the emotional and relational aspects of their development.

I do not wish to go into details but my biological family was a dysfunctional one; the family home was filled with much strife and occasional violence. There was a generational cycle I needed to break free from, and I needed spiritual intervention—healing from God and repentance on my part. I was wounded and trapped, hurt and hurting others. I brought dysfunctionality into my marriage and parenting, knowingly and unknowingly. On the fathering front, I was irresponsible, incompetent and negligent.

I thought I understood how to be a good father. I provided my children the affection and affirmation I never had when I was young. When my two sons were young, I would play and wrestle with them and bring them out to places of interest for fun activities during weekends.

However, as they grew older, I didn't teach them survival or communication skills. I wasn't much of a role model in these areas either. Also, like most traditional Asian parents, I shied away from educating or talking to my children about their sexuality because it was culturally embarrassing. I left it to my children to find their own way to educate themselves on it, outsourcing this seemingly taboo subject to the schools, the church, and their peers.

Though my son had occasional emotional outbursts in his teenage years about how he felt neglected and rejected, my wife and I barely suspected that he had struggles with same-sex attraction (SSA). For all the years that I'd raised my son, I'd known him to be a good boy with a kind and gentle spirit and a heart for the poor and needy. It was during my son's enlistment for national service that his struggle with SSA came to light. His military medical officer informed us of his sexual inclinations and struggles, and that he was found to be unsuitable for regular basic combat training.

The news came as a bombshell to us. Having known my son as an innocent, docile and obedient teenager, it felt like he was suddenly a different person. It broke my heart to know that he had been suppressing his feelings all this time, not feeling comfortable enough to share his struggles with me, not thinking that I could understand or protect him. It also made me realize how he must have had suffered rejection and hurt since his schooling years. From that point on, he adopted an avoidant, distrustful attitude towards us, growing distant and detached from us.

But that was just the start of bitter challenges he would face. Shortly after, he took a step of boldness to disclose his sexuality struggles to his church leaders. Unfortunately, this was met with judgement, rejection, and condemnation, instead of the needed empathy, acceptance, and help. He left his church and became a recluse at home, locking himself up in the room. He became guarded, distrustful, and defensive against any intrusion into his privacy, not wanting anyone to have access to his personal belongings, including his handphone, computer, or his social contacts.

In the months after he left church, abnormal behavioural patterns began to emerge. He became very withdrawn and disinterested in people, didn't seem to have much zest for life, and slowly adopted anti-establishment views. He was put on a weekly dosage of anti-depressants after seeing the army psychiatrist. As parents, we were duly worried. What was going on in our son's life and thoughts? Was he experiencing some kind of breakdown, disorientation, or insanity? Would he catch HIV and give up his faith altogether? Though we tried our best to talk to him about our concerns, it was mostly met with resistance and avoidance.

Hurt and rejected by the church, my son turned elsewhere to find relational and emotional support—finding solace in organisations that embraced his SSA as an inborn and acceptable way of life. His worldview started to change as he attended counselling by gay organizations and connected with gay friends on social media.

When my son dropped out of church, my wife and I—who were having a tumultuous marriage then—realized we needed to do something about it. Together, we decided to renew and strengthen our marriage vows, desiring to become better at protecting and shepherding our children. The first step involved saying sorry—to one another as well as to our children for the way we had neglected them and failed in our roles as parents. "Sorry" used to be the hardest word to say to one another but we now say it often because we value our marriage and family more than anything else.

The next thing we did was to attend a sexuality seminar where the speaker shared her moving testimony of how she surrendered her son to God, like Abraham placing Isaac on the altar. Like most parents struggling in this area, we have lost count of the many sleepless nights we have had agonising and praying, finding a way of sanctification and restoration. Surrendering our son to God was probably one of the hardest lessons to learn in this journey, but learning to do so has not only changed our perspective, it has changed us. Knowing that God loves him far more than we do, we entrust his destiny to God. But perhaps the biggest lesson we learned was the need for us, as prodigal children of God, to return to Him first and allow ourselves to be vessels of God to convey the Father's love to our son.

In the meantime, we will keep loving him no matter what. He is a precious gift from God. Ultimately, love is what he needs, love is the only thing that will not fail, love is the only lifeline we have and desperately cling to, and love is the only thing that can bring him back to us.

After all, is there any sin that can disqualify us from being part of the church—a community of brokenness—to be loved, restored and transformed? Who isn't a sinner himself that does not need to be understood, loved, and restored? Is there a spiritual leper whom Jesus does not want to reach out to touch and heal?

We believe that the parable of the prodigal son is a timeless story that can convict every heart and relate to every Christian in his redemptive journey back to God. Whatever sin and brokenness we are in, we are all prodigals finding our way home. We hope the church can come alongside to understand, accept and love these prodigals—just as God loves each one of us.

The Lord loves our son and family and has not given up on us. In fact, I have seen how my son has changed over the years. Though he is not yet ready to go back to church, He is now more willing to open up to us, and even joins us for regular family outings on a weekly basis. We must be the church to him and continue to affirm all that is good and praiseworthy in him.

We continue to pray and eagerly await the day when he will return to walk steadily with the God he once trusted and loved.

Tan Wei Chong

JOURNEYING IN HOPE
– Reflection –

When I first heard about this *Bruised Reeds* book project, I was excited. I wanted to meet and hear about the experiences of other Christians who had journeyed with individuals struggling with same-sex attraction (SSA). But after the initial meeting, I decided I was not going to contribute a story to this section. I felt that the journeys I had the privilege to be on with SSA friends didn't have enough resolution. My friends were still struggling. There was no "and they lived happily ever after" to speak of. What was there to testify to? So I agreed to write this reflection piece instead. I thought it would be easier to reflect on the successes of other people's stories.

There is an urgent need to equip the Body of Christ to walk with those who struggle with SSA. One common thread I discovered in reading these stories is a sense of helplessness. Many who journey with individuals struggling with SSA often report a sense of helplessness when the disclosure of SSA is made. They realize that there are many unknowns in journeying with an individual with SSA and there are few resources. Parents of individuals with SSA, in particular, feel the lack of support very keenly. Many are deeply affected by the discovery of their child's orientation and often internalize the struggle.

As I read through the contributions in this section, I began to realize, however, that I was not alone in feeling that I had not been able to help my SSA friends achieve their happily-ever-afters. In fact, I was actually in good company. None of the stories here have easy resolutions or neat answers. While Evans' and Jez's stories of their interactions with Val do contain a heterosexual marriage, the marriage per se is not the solution or conclusion of their journeys. These are all stories in progress. They are still unfolding narratives in the lives of those touched by SSA. This is perhaps a reflection of the lived reality of many individuals who struggle with SSA and those who journey with them.

Typically, the meta-narrative of testimonies one might hear in church are those of having overcome a particular sin, temptation, or area of brokenness. As eager as we are (and should be) to showcase the victories that Christ has given us in our lives, the danger of telling only such stories is that those who are still in the midst of their struggles may feel that their stories cannot be shared—not until they have tasted some recognizable victory. Therefore, for many who struggle with SSA and those who journey with them, this may feel very far out of reach.

Broken but Faithful
Wesley Hill is a theologian; he also describes himself as a gay, celibate Christian. Zondervan (who published his book, *Washed and Waiting*) describes his journey in the book's blurb as "faithfulness in the midst of brokenness". That phrase has stuck with me ever since I first read it. Until we see God face-to-face and experience glorification, we are all still imperfect creatures who live in a sin-stained world. Our Christian journeys are all stories of "faithfulness in the midst of brokenness".

Vulnerable Authenticity

Church leaders can help those struggling with SSA by fostering a culture of vulnerability and authenticity in their churches. One key way they can do this is by sharing their own struggles of brokenness and pain. Unfortunately, when it comes to sexuality, there is already a strong taboo in the Singapore Church. On the topic of SSA, this taboo is intensified. We need leaders who are willing to set the tone. When you go first, it gives others the permission to go second. It opens a safe space for others to share. Perhaps what is challenging in being vulnerable is that to do so, we first need to confront those areas of brokenness in our own lives—issues we would rather deny, ignore or downplay. In her friendship with Joe and his partner Ben, Eunice shares how God began to uncover her own sin and brokenness. Her weaknesses allowed Joe and Ben to become instruments of God's love to her.

There is also something else we should be aware of. When talking about SSA in church, we often employ the language of "us" versus "them". Sometimes, consciously or unconsciously, we wield this kind of divisive rhetoric as a weapon, in a misguided attempt to hammer the LGBTQ community into moral submission. As the stories in this book show, there is no "us" versus "them"; individuals with SSA are already in the church. While this happens to be the hot-button topic in the present culture wars, we must be careful and gracious in the way we communicate about SSA to the church. For those of us who are heterosexual, we need to relinquish our tendency to see our heterosexuality as making us somehow superior to those struggling witrh SSA. Sexual purity is an ethical demand for all who profess faith in Christ. But we rarely call heterosexuals to the same standards of sexual purity that we insist for our same-sex attracted friends. We need to admit that we all struggle with brokenness.

Life-giving Spiritual Friendships

The context for grappling with our brokenness is Christian community. The practice of spiritual friendship has been neglected in our highly individualistic Christian culture. We need to reclaim this practice of deep, sacrificial relationships in the Body of Christ. Many of the stories in this section illuminate the value of such relationships. In journeying with Sara and Bella, Amanda realized that she was not expected to "fix" them. Instead, she only needed to be a friend. In my ministry with young adults, I have observed that many do not know how to be genuine friends with one another—they may have grown up in church with one another, but their friendships remain at a superficial social level.

The United Kingdom has appointed a Minister for Loneliness, an acknowledgement of how pervasive loneliness is in society. Yet loneliness is rarely acknowledged by the faithful. Individuals with SSA feel this isolation even more keenly. We need to cultivate friendships where there is empathy and unconditional regard. The struggle with SSA is a long road; it may even be for life. Thus advice-giving or providing quick-fix solutions is often not loving nor useful. It would be better to cry with someone with SSA than try to "cure" them.

At the same time, we ought to be careful about singling out individuals with SSA for special treatment—either positive or negative. As Lenda wrote, "Sometimes walking with people with same-sex attraction is just like walking with any other person." Constance realized in her friendship with Yen that she had been treating him with kid-gloves, reluctant to confront his bad habits. Individuals with SSA need avenues to serve and exercise their God-given spiritual gifts too. Linda's friend, Eric, serves in various ministries in church and is a godparent. One's orientation does not define one's identity in Christ.

Already but Not Yet

Whether attracted to the same sex or the opposite one, our shared goal as Christians is to pursue God and grow more in His image. What we need to do is to open up a space in the garden of Christian community, an image Carrie offers in her story—a space that allows the Gardener to work.

Many of these "best practices" highlighted here do not only benefit those who struggle with SSA. They help to make the church an improved version of itself—a better place for all who struggle with brokenness. While support groups (such as the one that enabled Aldrin to meet other parents) can be immensely helpful, they are only one part of a bigger picture. The larger Body must be engaged in the broader work of creating a safe space to work out faithfulness in the midst of brokenness.

Our eschatology must be balanced—we live in the tension between what theologians call the "already but not yet". Because Christ has already come, we have victory over sin, disease and death. But because the kingdom has not yet come in its fullness, we will still sin, suffer, and die. It should not surprise us then when individuals with SSA are not "cured"—there is much that is still "not yet" in their lives and in ours. At the same time, we hold out for the hope that one day He will wipe every tear from our eyes, and there will be no more death or mourning or crying or pain, a day when the old order of things will have passed away, a time when He will have made all things new! We are all waiting for the end of the story, for all things to be made happily ever after forever. Until that day, we labour, live, and journey in hope.

Marianne Wong
Pastoral Assistant
Youth & Young Adults Ministry
Mt Carmel Bible-Presbyterian Church

SECTION 3 — CREATING COMMUNITY

A SAME-SEX ATTRACTED PASTOR'S JOURNEY

I am a pastor in Singapore who discovered my same-sex attraction (SSA) during my teenage years.

I am a testimony of God's grace. I was never abandoned by God in my journey with SSA. I have kept the faith and pursued a full-time vocational Christian calling. Now, I am happily married with three children. Because of my journey, I have a "bi-focal" perspective of SSA from the lens of a church member with SSA as well as from the lens of a pastor. I am able to reflect on what it is like to journey with SSA both personally and pastorally.

I have counselled many with SSA. From my experience, I have made three key reflections. My desire is to share them with pastors and other church leaders so that they can minister to those with SSA in the church more effectively. The greatest battle concerning SSA is not outside the church, but inside the church.

Find Opportunities to Share Sexual Struggles as a Pastor

Change begins at the top. As the saying goes, monkey see, monkey do. In this postmodern age, congregation members need more than rhetoric. They need to see rhetoric *and* redemption in the lives of their leaders. Pastors need to take the risk of being authentic before their members, though they need to do it wisely. I am not advocating that pastors share their deepest sexual struggles over the pulpit, or hold a sexuality emphasis month in their church. But on certain occasions, church members need to hear the sexuality struggles of their leaders, because as leaders share their journey authentically, members will follow.

I grew up in a traditional church where the pastor was seen as a priestly authority figure. When my SSA emerged while I was a teenager, I was full of anxiety and loneliness. I felt as if I was the only one who struggled with sexual issues. It would take ten years before I could find a safe platform to share my secret struggle. Part of the reluctance was the fact that none of the church leaders talked about sexuality.

When I began exploring full-time church ministry work, I really struggled with whether I should tell my colleagues and my Senior Pastor. I struggled for many reasons. First and foremost, I wanted people to know me as a person, not as a person who struggled with SSA.

> In almost every situation, I never felt judged or looked down upon. In fact, the exact opposite happened. People were encouraged and began to openly share about their own struggles.

Slowly, over the period of many years, almost half of my colleagues and about half of my small group came to know about my background. In almost every situation, I never felt judged or looked down upon. In fact, the exact opposite happened. People were encouraged and began to openly share about their own struggles. If we want to see people become more open about their sexuality struggles, the leadership should share their own journey. That is why I am so grateful that in our church, we have an encouraging and authentic men's ministry where people can be open about these issues.

Understand the Unique Issues Faced by Those with SSA
I often hear such phrases in church: "Hate the sin, love the sinner" and "SSA is just like any other sin". While these statements may be true, they are inadequate. Both fail to reflect an understanding of the unique situation faced by those with SSA. Yes, having SSA might lead to sin, but there is tremendous social stigma attached to SSA as compared to other sins. There is no social agenda, for example, to give equal rights and accept those who struggle with materialism, anger, or jealousy. And most Christians and non-Christians alike would agree that watching pornography and committing adultery are clearly sins. But the struggle with SSA is not so straightforward. Often, the media tells us to accept SSA while the church tells us to reject it. We need to create a church culture that acknowledges this tension.

I have found these three categories helpful to meet the needs of those with SSA in our church:

Those who are not ready to share. We cannot force those who have SSA to open up. Even in the most transparent environments, there are people who won't share for various reasons. We can only wait for the Lord to touch their hearts through the Word or through the testimony of other people.

Those who are ready to share, but don't know whom to share with. We should identify leaders such as small group leaders, counsellors, and pastors for people to approach to share their sexual struggles. People rarely share such deep struggles before or after Sunday worship. In my experience, people usually confide such issues during men-only or women-only retreats, or during camps.

Those who are ready to share, but who give up half-way through the counselling process. I am a firm believer that counselling is effective for those with SSA. Unfortunately, there are many who drop out along the way. I have experienced that for every five persons who share with me, only two keep in contact with me. The retention rate is low because oftentimes, both the counsellor and counsellee are not clear what "victory" looks like for someone with SSA. Is the goal heterosexuality or bisexuality? Is it to manage temptations? Is it abstinence? Or marriage? If these answers are not clear, discouragement and disillusionment cause people to stop the counselling journey. The end goal, which is common to all believers, is a Christ-mastered disciple—whether married or single. It is not freedom from SSA attractions, but the freedom to willingly die to self and to live for Christ.

Integrate People with SSA into the Larger Church Community

SSA should not be a lonely discipleship journey.

Intentionality in helping those with SSA integrate into a wider community is critical. I once had a person share his SSA journey privately with me. It was a beneficial session. But after the session, I asked that his small-group leader join our next session. This is a necessary and intentional step as it requires the one struggling with SSA to confide in another person in the church. The purpose of having the small-group leader attend is two-fold: To educate the leader about the SSA journey, and to provide an additional level of support beyond the pastor. Most are reluctant, as they desire to keep their struggle a private one. I have never once had a small-group leader refuse to come alongside a member with SSA. Without the small-group leader's involvement, the sessions would remain a counsellor-to-counsellee relationship. Expanding the span of care is critical for reducing the shame and for increasing the support. I encourage those with SSA to find at least one or two friends (in their small group, if they are part of one) to be part of the healing journey.

Let me share briefly regarding the role of para-church ministries ministering to those with SSA. I am not negating the ministry of SSA recovery and support groups. They provide specialized counselling and equipping that many churches do not have. However, what I have found is that church leaders tend to send their members to these recovery groups but, when they complete their sessions and return to their home churches, no one knows what has occurred, because the recovery was done *outside* the church family.

When recovery occurs in isolation, there is a great chance that an SSA sub-culture will be created in the church, where the SSA struggler shares only with other SSA stragglers. This is not a healthy situation, because this will create a larger gap between those with SSA and those without. This will simply perpetuate the culture that we have in many churches today where we are de facto closed to ministering to those with SSA.

It is my prayer that one day, before we return home to Jesus, there will be no distinction between those with SSA and those without and that those who struggle with SSA will testify, with all the saints, that Jesus is the way, the truth, and the life (John 14:6).

Andrew Cho
Pastor

RESTORING THE BROKEN

I came to know the Lord 25 years ago. In these 25 years of my pilgrimage with Jesus Christ, He led me to know several brothers who struggled deeply with same-sex attraction (SSA), and used those friendships to teach me precious lessons and to shape my life and pastoral ministry. I would like to share some of these key lessons that I learnt and am still learning.

When I first became a member of the local church that I've been a part of ever since, a brother in his early 40s befriended me and reached out to me to encourage me, a young Christian. His warm and friendly personality was an encouragement to many, but as I got to know him more personally, I discovered that his external sociability belied a person who had suffered many setbacks, resulting in his suffering chronic pessimism in his thoughts, and deep pain in his heart. After two major brain surgeries, he lived with recurring depression and would often lament about how life had dealt him a bad deck of cards. By the grace of God, our friendship grew as we spent much time together, often on a weekly basis, to the point where he would invite me to stay overnight at his place. Soon he began to ask me to sleep next to him whenever I stayed over, and he would like to hold my hand when sleeping. Even though I felt uncomfortable at first (as I had never related so closely to a brother physically), I did not give much thought to it until one day, he divulged to me that he had been struggling with SSA since youth. This revelation helped me to make sense of his emotional dependency on brothers, his physical expressions of affection towards me and his pursuit of male friendships. The Lord used this understanding to help me to begin to understand that his SSA struggles were merely symptomatic of his deeper need for male bonding, brotherly love and healthy male friendships, things that had been lacking in his life. By the grace of God, the Lord enabled me to continue relating and reaching out to him as a brother in Christ. Unfortunately, ever since he revealed to me his deepest secret, he lived in the fear that I would betray his confidence. He was plagued by the constant fear that he would be found out. Some years later, to the shock of my life, I received the news that he had committed suicide. The years of the mental anguish of living with the shame, fear and pain of struggling with SSA had finally taken their toll. In my eight years of friendship with him, the Lord taught me that those who struggle with SSA primarily need safe relationships where they can experience unconditional love and acceptance. They need this in order to grow healthily in relational bonding and friendships with the same gender, indeed, to grow into the image of God.

In the same period, the Lord led me to know two other brothers with SSA. The first was a fellow church brother named JT whom I was discipling in the context of a university Christian discipleship group. We have been journeying together for the past 23 years, growing from a disciple-maker and disciple relationship, to a brotherly friendship, to being partners in Christ reaching out to brothers with SSA. In the initial years of our discipleship relationship, JT not only shared with me his pains of struggling with SSA but also his brokenness of growing up without his father's strength and affirming influence. He had been bullied by his schoolmates, who labelled him a girlie, and was sexually abused by his army instructor. The Lord taught me that like any other behavioural problems and relational pains that we have in this world, SSA is just another consequence of the effects of sin in the fallen world that we live in. In this case, it included the sin of ungodly fathering, the sin of not according the due respect and dignity to a fellow human being created in the image of God, and the sin of sexual abuse. As a result, the Lord began to teach me how to be a spiritual father to JT, to relate with him in the Heavenly Father's gracious love instead of in my own fleshly and legalistic expectations. I learnt to relate to him just as I would to other brothers as one loved by God, whose identity and dignity is found in Jesus Christ alone. I learnt to grow together with JT and to mutually encourage each other in our journey to live in sexual purity together. I too constantly battled with my own struggles with sexual sins, with my own experiences of defeat and bondage. And in this pilgrimage of growing in Christ together, the Lord is now leading us to be partners in His ministry of reaching out to other men struggling with sexual brokenness.

Amazingly, the Lord taught me many of these precious lessons about ministering to people with SSA through a personal friend who became my mentor in the early years of my Christian life. We met in university and he was a model of godliness, servant leadership and disciple-making. I saw in him the reality of Christ-likeness in the way he walked with the Lord, related with others, expressed love toward me, and discipled men, and in his service to God. All this was despite his challenges. The Lord blessed our friendship and we became best pals. I have looked up to him as my mentor and the person who had the most in-fluence on my Christian life to date. It was only much later in our friendship when he shared with me about his own personal struggles with SSA. In spite of that, he remained my best buddy and mentor. I am eternally grateful to the Lord for blessing my life with his ministry. Because of him, I learned that in the grace of God, the Lord saves us to live lives for His glory. He uses us for his wonderful purposes to bless others in spite of our personal struggles and bat-tles so that we will know that it is all about Him. It is the abounding love and grace of our Lord Jesus Christ that makes all the difference. He works in and through our lives for the glory of our Heavenly Father by the power of the Holy Spirit. This is my story as an offering of thanksgiving to the Lord and a tribute to the beloved brothers whom the Lord has sent into my life to bless me.

Finally, in my pilgrimage I also learnt that I am called to shepherd the church to reach out to people struggling with sexual brokenness and to disciple them. By the grace of God, since last year our church has started a support group ministry to reach out to men struggling with SSA related challenges. I am learning that for the Lord to equip His church to reach out to people with sexual brokenness, the following principles and practices are vital:

> 1. The lead pastor must be an example. He must model authenticity and brokenness to the church. He must help establish a safe environment for the church to become a community where people can form safe relationships where they are able to confess their sins, and share with one another about their deepest darkness and struggles. In such communities they can receive God's grace, love,

encouragement, and even discipline as they pursue Christ together. To build such a safe community, the Lord led me to share openly with my leaders and congregation about my own struggles, bondages and deliverance from porn addiction, and other challenges in my life.

2.   The church has to be equipped to reach out to and disciple men and women with sexual broken-ness. For that to happen, we began to trust God to establish the men's and women's ministry in the church. In our case we had to prayerfully select and appoint lay people burdened with God's calling to disciple men and women to lead these ministries.

3.   Furthermore, these servant leaders had to be equipped for effective disciple-making of men and women seeking to pursue Jesus Christ out of sexual brokenness. For them to be effective, I saw the need to teach them through modelling—how to relate to people with God's unconditional acceptance, to in-vest in intentional friendship, to represent Christ to them, and to disciple them by showing them how to walk with the Holy Spirit so that they could grow in the knowledge of their true identity in Christ. They needed to know that their real satisfaction was to be found in Him, the fountain of living water, and then to go help others make the same discovery.

Hon Chin Foang
Lead Pastor
Good News Baptist Church

STRUGGLING FOR CHANGE

The first time it hit me was around ten years ago. I awoke one morning to a series of very startling messages that my fellow church leader from years past had married another man and had announced it on social media. I was shocked, then angry. Not so much angry at the broadcast, but angry that despite the years of close fellowship and intense Bible study, he hadn't shared a thing with any of us. We were blindsided. But then again, should I really have been surprised? After all, I hadn't mentioned my serious pornography and masturbation addiction to any of them either. Was I any different from him? How could it be that both of us (and I'm sure many others), in one of the greatest evangelical churches in the UK, at the presumed peak of our spiritual zeal, methodically studying the Scriptures, could not share the struggles and sinful behaviour that took place behind closed doors? This left a deep wound.

Fast forward a few years, to when I had become a pastor. What would this mean for MY church congregation? I was determined not to allow such things to fester. In my new role, one of the first things I started was a sexual addiction "anonymous" group. It was called a 3XA group. This involved a few guys meeting weekly over the course of one to two years, using material called *Pure Eyes*. We shared our sins openly and learned terms like "triggers" and "accountability". I ran a couple of these groups over the course of three years. Most shared about heterosexual struggles with pornography and masturbation, one or two about their homosexual or bisexual inclinations.

However, after the first two rounds I decided to stop. Why? Firstly, the groups were immensely draining on me personally—I felt that I had to shoulder their burdens on my own. There was no one willing to co-lead.

Furthermore, talking weekly about sexual things (in some detail) made me always think of sexual things. It was already not healthy for me; was it healthy for them? But more importantly, I wondered if the group was helping at all. Weekly failures, the same failures, for one to two years straight—was there any point? The guys told me it was doing them good—I wasn't too sure, it felt pretty hopeless. I considered it a failure and, to their dismay, shelved the project.

So what next? I didn't know, I just left it to God. I carried on with normal ministry—preaching, teaching, and lots of Bible study (we are talking about a BIBLE-Presbyterian church after all!).

Leaving it to God was probably the best "idea" I had. As I continued to study the Scriptures, I became convicted of two key ingredients necessary for illumination and transformation. The first was "gospel safety". A sharing of one's failures—or to use the Christian expression, a confession of sins—requires a deep level of assurance that one will not be met with condemnation, but rather grace. If the gospel was not strongly and powerfully taught, people would not come forward to confess in response—and those that did, only in a cathartic way. I realized that the 3XA groups had only allowed for a temporary emotional release, but it didn't seem to go deeper than that. The confession had to be triggered by the "bravery" that came from deeply experiencing the work of Christ's cross.

The second was that the person doing the teaching needed to be a person who embodied the Word. When we ran the 3XA groups, one of the required steps was to find a person that they could be accountable to. Interestingly, all the guys in the groups independently chose the same two to three Christians, despite being in a 1000-people church! They were all leaders whom the group members felt (1) could teach the gospel—they were mature and able; (2) understood sin—they had vulnerability and humility; and (3) embodied grace—they shared warmth and safety. None of these people were experts in sexuality, nor had they a known history of ministering to people with sexual addictions—but it seemed they were the right people to go to! I later also realized that the only reason guys came to share about their SSA struggles with me was not because I had ever preached a single word about SSA, but because I too seemingly embodied similar characteristics. Maybe the type of sin didn't matter—it could be sexual issues, gambling problems, alcohol abuse—they all went to the same people for help. Sexual sins are deep sins, but they are still sins. Sexual sinners are not "them", they are us, and all of us need the same kind of gospel help.

Convinced of this, I then decided what we needed was not to run an SSA ministry or more "professional" 3XA groups. The church needed a cultural change. We—the existing leaders—needed to become the kinds of people that those struggling with some form of debilitating dark-ness could go to in confidence.

Step 1—Do we as leaders even confess our sins to one another? Do we have such gospel confidence? Well I wasn't going to ask the entire Board of Elders to start openly confessing their sins—that's not really a good way to make friends. But we could start by meeting up with one another outside of ministry events and business meetings. We started the "Quad" system—where one pastor and three elders would meet up monthly to read God's Word and to share how we were doing. This was later given better language when Rev Tan Soo Inn shared with us his 3-2-1 method, where 3 Christians agree to meet up, 2 hourly, once (1) a month to share openly and pray deeply about all aspects of life—work, ministry and family. We did this with the Elders, then the Staff, then opened it up to the whole church to be done in all the small groups—voluntarily of course. After a couple of years, you could tangibly feel the difference in how the leaders talked to one another. It was refreshing.

Step 2—Do we as leaders confess our sins to the congregation, where appropriate? This was going to be a LOT harder! I was already privileged to have a senior pastor who did not hide his mistakes. When something went wrong administratively, he was brave enough to apologize publicly—a great example. I decided that I would find avenues to talk about sins, even *my* past and present sins in appropriate and helpful ways—to various segments of the congregation. There was the occasional sermon where I would share about my past pornography addiction, and my present struggles with pride and feelings of inadequacy. There were other sermons where I thought it was more helpful to use humour and creative means to get hidden sins out in the open. For example, during a Galatians 6 sermon, I acted out a skit of a young man trying to open up about his sexual addictions. The comedy cut through the obvious tension, making it easier to talk about the sin. Again, this was something I learned from my senior pastor who had written a book called *Make them Laugh, Help them Learn.* Plus, of course, looking at the near-lunatic drama of the ancient prophets when they wanted to get a point across! Using the pulpit, small groups, special classes, and social media, I got others to share their testimony of weakness from the angles of mental health, fears of singleness, parenting woes, and marital struggles. The issues had to be hit at multiple levels using all means available. Some of it was purposeful, most times simply opportunistic, as God brought the people or programmes onto my radar.

But again, I stress, the best decision was to leave these things to God. He then brought in something I had perhaps given up looking for? A tool to come alongside someone stuck in relational or sexual brokenness. This was "Journey".[1]

I found a random course in the Biblical Graduate School of Theology called "Spiritual Healing". The thing that intrigued me was that the teacher was a flamenco dancer! I

---

1   Journey Singapore is a community-based, Christ-centred discipleship ministry that exists to help people find hope and live life through experiencing Jesus in their relationships and sexuality. (http://journeysingapore.org)

then realized that the course was actually a part of a larger worldwide programme to aid those in deep darkness, using prayer and discipleship. I had never experienced something so personally liberating and sustaining. I was sold and wanted to do everything to be part of this—first for my own sake, and later to bring this back to Zion Bishan. God opened all the doors—it was quite stunning. I'm still a Journey newbie, but I know that this was His answer to my decade-old question, and it made me so much more hopeful in terms of my spiritual growth. There was hope—yes, there IS hope—and it was embodied so vividly by the "Journey International" leaders who were walking pictures of brokenness being healed. "Journey" is not the only tool out there, but it was the tool that God brought to me and addressed my circumstance, here and now—"Journey" and Luke's Gospel. Why Luke's Gospel? Well, that's a story for another day.

If you are someone struggling with SSA or other sexual issues, I pray you may meet some people transformed by the gospel, and hopefully equipped with healing tools like "Journey". Then maybe, just maybe, they will be able to walk with you, just like someone is walking with them. You will find these people in any gospel-centred church. Ask God to show them to you—He loves to answer that prayer.

Dev Menon
Pastor
Zion Bishan Bible-Presbyterian Church

RECKLESS LOVE STORIES

was torn inside as I contemplated the fact that I had to share one of my deepest, darkest secrets with the world.

"Ian, Ian, would you share your story to the church?" came this soundless voice one night. This God-thought jolted me out of my dream state. "What story?" I feigned ignorance. Surely God didn't mean that story, the story I had hidden in the secret safe that was tucked away in the depths of my heart. In fact I had long since thrown away the key to that safe.

"I will not share that story, God."

How could I share the account of me being sexually abused at the tender age of five? I started having flashbacks to my younger five-year-old self. After that molestation, I found myself sexually awakened prematurely. I also remembered how my father had caught me touching myself inappropriately and had punished me harshly, but that didn't stop me from slipping into a lifestyle of chronic masturbation. Things got worse when I found myself helplessly addicted to pornography.

Remembering my father's harsh reaction to my childhood masturbation, I realized that it would not be easy for the church to come to terms with my personal journey of pornographic addiction. Would Lilis, my wife, be ready and supportive when the story came out? Besides, my church—3:16 Church—was an infant, barely six months old. Were we ready for such vulnerability and raw sharing? What if people were so disturbed by what was shared that they left the church?

God really loves to move in the spaces of my questions and doubts. You may be surprised by the things that I do not know, even as a senior pastor. But God often fills in our empty spaces with divine suggestions that lead us to fresh revelations. At other times, He leads me to undertake a project, and, in the course of learning to obey, He reveals and engraves intimate answers into my heart. Walking with the heavenly Father, I often feel like a child despite being the senior pastor of a young, vibrant church. But I *am* His child. My spiritual father once said to me, "Ian, grow but do not grow up. Because the kingdom belongs to those who are like a child."

In God's own gentle and mysterious ways, He worked slowly but surely in Lilis' heart and in mine. I felt like I was losing to God in this divine game of tug of war. I found myself beginning to want to obey His prompting. There were invisible heavenly strings pulling at my heart to share. It felt more and more like God was setting me up to model what love may look like in 3:16 Church. He was teaching me that shame dies when stories can be shared in safe places.

In the midst of preparing my story, it dawned on me that God was going to use it to teach the church how to create a safe environment for broken people, a safe space—so rare in our modern society—where people will not feel condemned, where they can be vulnerable, yet know that they are deeply loved to the core for who they really are.

After much thoughtful contemplation and in discussion with Lilis, we felt that we were finally ready to open our inner hearts. We were ready to share with the church what we had held sacred and had only kept within the family. On 16 June 2013, Lilis and I took a leap of faith and shared our story of sexual brokenness at a Sunday Service. I almost did not dare to look into the faces of the people in the congregation, knowing that among them were friends, family, and others who had left my previous church to set up 3:16 Church with me. I felt that as we laid our story on holy ground, it was an act of worship to God. It was an eternal pledge of love to the church as we surrendered our story to our loving Father.

Something in the spiritual realm broke that day! A few significant things happened to 3:16 Church after we shared and we knew that our lives had been changed forever.

The floodgates of powerful testimonies opened, and a greater level of healing and strengthening was released in the church. Here are a few examples: A sister shared about the marital struggles that she had carried with her for over ten years and had never opened up about to anyone in church before. A brother shared publicly about his journey of experiencing same-sex attraction (SSA). Another sister opened up about her life of promiscuity, and how she was adamant about giving that up as she followed Jesus.

But as much as our sharing did good for the church, I came to realize that God ultimately wanted me to share it for my own healing, because He loves me.

After the service, my father came up to me in tears. I could not tell if those were tears of relief or regret, or both. I was shaken as I had never seen my father in that state before. I was afraid of what he would say next. He shared with me how shocked he was that I could still remember the incident when he had punished me harshly, which had happened when I was five. He had not realized how that incident could be so pivotal and defining for a young boy. He remembered that incident now and then, and it had always been something that haunted him.

My father told me that my sharing gave him closure as well. Little did I know it was a wound for him as much as it was for me. We had not spoken for so many years. God has this amazing tender-loving way of surfacing the forgotten thorns lodged in our hearts. In His perfect time, He redeemed those wounds and helped bring reconciliation, a healing that could not have happened without His love. We cried so much that day as we helped each other to forgive. I could feel the embrace of the heavenly Father and the Son of God over both of us! We shared this story in detail in 2017 on Youtube.[1]

Honestly, when 3:16 Church was founded, I did not know that it was the Senior Pastor's job to provide a safe environment conducive for healing and growth. I thought that my job was just to pray and to preach the Word. The Holy Spirit convicted me that that was not enough, because the Word will only have power when it is made flesh. Apostle Paul said, "I want you to pattern your lives after me, just as I pattern mine after Christ." (1 Corinthians 11:1, The Pas-

---

1   https://www.youtube.com/watch?v=6A8RaoMsG8c

sion Translation) It is imperative that pastors live what they teach and preach. We leaders can only reproduce another generation of leaders by our example.

The importance of cultivating a healthy church culture is not taught much in Bible seminaries. A healthy church culture is one where people are authentic, not fake.

Imagine walking into the Singapore Botanic Gardens and finding it filled with plasticky, fake flowers and artificial grass where mother nature's presence is clearly lacking. No fluttering of the colourful wings of the butterflies, no chirping of the birds that sound like music to our ears, no buzzing of the bees as they harvest the sweet nectar of the blossoming flowers. Such a garden is lifeless, fake and cold, far from what God had in mind when He created the world to be a blessing to humankind.

A healthy church culture always advances the gospel and strengthens the work of disciple-making. This is extremely important because we experience wonders and miracles when God uses broken people to heal broken people. And this is only possible in a safe space where leaders set an example of vulnerability. This encourages people to come out and be vulnerable themselves. The glory of God is best shown in stories of grace. And aren't we all to be walking evidence of the goodness of God?

Culture is invisible and yet it impacts everything. I began to read the Bible and the Holy Spirit opened my eyes to see that God was the first Culturist! He *is* the Master Atmosphere Architect and the Chief Environment Engineer. He created an amazing universe and planted mankind in a Paradisal Garden.

"Then the LORD God took the man and put him into the garden of Eden to cultivate it and keep it." Genesis 2:5

Interestingly, Adam, the first man on earth, was also given the responsibility to tenderly cultivate the land and to tend the garden. Pastors too have a sacred calling to tend the spiritual garden of God's people. Pastors are to feed the sheep and to take care of them. We are to equip the saints for the work of God. The church owes the world an authentic witness to Jesus, whose life can only be seen in those who are healed, helped, and filled with the love of the Father.

What I have learnt through all this is that the sharing of honest stories creates safe spaces! When a Senior Pastor can come out to share his story of brokenness and redemption in safety in his church, his church is truly a safe space and it sets a beautiful precedent for others to do the same.

Ian Toh
Senior Pastor
3:16 Church

COMING OUT AND GOING IN

"Fear not, for you will not be ashamed; be not confounded, for you will not be disgraced; for you will forget the shame of your youth, and the reproach of your widowhood you will remember no more." Isaiah 54:4 (ESV)

I froze in my seat, struck dumb by the still small voice that whispered this verse into my heart. It was clear that God was speaking to me …

It was September 2013. I was attending a two-day seminar conducted by Liberty League. I was there with my pastoral team, seeking to learn how to minister to the sexually broken. On the second day of the seminar, I sat in the auditorium listening to the testimonies of various speakers. I was moved by their willingness to bare their scars before men. It struck me that it took a lot of courage and humility for them to openly share their sexual brokenness with us.

Suddenly, the verse in Isaiah 54:4 floated into my memory. And the Spirit spoke: "Son, these who spoke are my beloved children and I am not ashamed of them. I will also remove their shame and reproach, and they will remember them no more." I came to understand that God intended to redeem their sexual brokenness and weave them into the grand tapestry of His redemptive story! As I sat there overwhelmed by this revelation in the Spirit, I began to praise God in my heart. But the Spirit continued to speak to me: "Son, it's time for me to do the same for you too. It is time to deal with those skeletons in the closet. I will remove the shame of your youth. I will redeem your shame for My glory." I trembled and broke down in tears...

A few days later, I sat at the kitchen table with my wife and in tears sought her forgiveness for hiding my sexual brokenness from her. I told her of my past struggle with my sexual identity. I confessed my periodic struggle with addictions to pornography and masturbation to her. I was ready to face the music. She had every right to be angry and to reject me since I had not been truthful with her from day one of our marriage. My wife, however, responded with compassion which I didn't deserve. Instead of berating me, she actually felt pained that I had to bear this secret shame alone for so long. What grace!

A week later, I confessed to the elders of the church and sought their forgiveness for not being truthful to them when they were seeking to appoint me as the pastor of the church. I was ready to lose my job. I knew they had every right to dismiss me immediately for not disclosing my sexual sins and brokenness when I entered the pastorate. The elders, however, responded in love. They wept alongside me as I confessed my sins and brokenness before them and they hugged me to assure me of their love. What grace again!

In my coming out, I was ready to be rejected by men. I held on to Isaiah 54:4. Being accepted by God was all that mattered to me. Knowing that God has not rejected me and that He will one day remove my shame and reproach granted me courage and motivation to come to the light and not allow the devil to keep me in the dark dungeon of secret shame any longer.

After coming out to my wife and the elders of the church, I found courage to come out to my children. In God's beautiful timing, my pre-teen son asked me one night (just a few days after I had confessed to my wife) whether I had struggled with pornography before. I confessed my addictions to him. My son then asked me to be his accountability partner! Since then, he has experienced no shame or fear in sharing with me his struggle with sexual temptations. What joy to have this open and transparent relationship with my son!

Knowing that there are many in the church who are privately struggling with sexual brokenness and addictions, I felt led to create a safe environment for them to come out and experience God's assurance of forgiveness and His power of redemption. I decided to come out to my congregation to help usher in that safe environment. I first shared my story with the brothers in a church camp. Thereafter, I shared it with the rest of the congregation during one of the church services. I also started a monthly support group for brothers struggling with sexual sins and brokenness. In the first few cycles, various brothers came to this support group. Some came to confess their past sexual sins, like engaging in one-night stands and visiting prostitutes. Brothers who struggled with pornography and masturbation came to confess their sin and seek accountability. Some of these brothers had unwanted same-sex attraction (SSA). I had the joy of witnessing some of these brothers experiencing definite victory over their battle against pornography and masturbation.

The structure of the support group is simple: it begins with a time of open confession (beginning with me) as we recount how the past month has been in terms of our sexual purity. This is followed by a time of reflecting over some content (e.g. articles, books, and videos) related to wholeness in Christ. Finally, we end the time with prayer and intercession.

After a few cycles, the support group began to focus on those who struggled with SSA. Some of these brothers have remained in the group for more than two years. I am privileged to be walking alongside them in this journey towards wholeness. This group of brothers has been God's instrument in helping me to grow in personal holiness.

Some precious lessons I have learnt in my journey of coming out of my secret shame and going in to walk with the sexually broken are:

1.   You Have to Come Out in Order to Go In

There are many leaders who are unable to effectively minister to those who are struggling with sexual sins or brokenness because they too are struggling with secret shame. When I had not yet come out, the devil muted my ministry in this domain. I found it difficult to minister to brothers who struggled with pornography. I felt like a hypocrite and the devil constantly accused me of my own personal failure. I therefore ministered from a distance, unable to come alongside effectively to help my brothers. After coming out, I was able to openly share about my own battle against sexual sins with these brothers. They also found courage to share their sexual failures with me knowing that they would not be rejected or stigmatized by me.

2.   You Have to Take the Lead

There is a saying that goes: "The speed of the leader, the speed of the congregation." How far a leader will go in his confession will set the benchmark for the members to follow. If the leader shares superficially, the members will not feel safe to share deeply. In the support group, I realize that how much each member will share is directly proportional to how much I am willing to make myself vulnerable before them. So I will always take the lead in the open confession time to set the right depth of sharing.

3.   Same-sex Lust—the Same, Yet Not the Same

Lust comes in different shapes. Some are more inclined to lust after material things, some are more inclined to lust after the opposite sex, while some lust after the same sex. Yet lust is lust. God does not rank sins, and all types of lust are equally displeasing to God. In this light, the sin of same-sex lust is no different from the sin of opposite-sex lust. It is good for those who struggle with SSA to know that their lusts do not warrant more punishment than other sins.

Nevertheless, the struggles of same-sex lust are different from those who struggle with opposite-sex temptations. This is because they also have to battle against existing social stigmas. In addition, social stereotyping of gender roles and behaviours isn't helpful. Therefore, many of them face intense shame and rejection compared to those who struggle with opposite-sex lust. We will do well not to generalize their struggles nor belittle their pain.

4.   SSA Goes Beyond the Sexual Front

Several I know struggle with past baggage in their lives. Many have suffered traumatic childhood abuses. Some had absent or dysfunctional fathers, some were molested when young and some were exposed to pornography and masturbation in their early years by irresponsible adults.

Many also experience emotional anguish due to the shame and rejection that they face regularly. Others struggle with loneliness as they think it is implausible that they could fall in love and marry someone they love.

Therefore, it would be naïve for one to think that those who struggle with SSA only face issues related to their sexuality. They also battle with relational wounds, emotional and mental scars and self-condemnation. The healing that they pursue is for their whole being and not just for their sexuality.

5. Many Believers Who Struggle with SSA are Holier than Those Who Don't

As mentioned, I usually begin the monthly support group with a time of open confession. You may think that it consists of "big-time" confessions where members in the group confess how each had committed homosexual acts with another stranger, etc. However, it is not. Most of the time, the confessions concern the entertaining of impure thoughts or the occasional fall into pornography or masturbation. For example, a brother will confess of two impure thoughts he entertained in the past month. Another will confess to watching a couple of M18 (with nudity or scenes of intimacy) video clips on a video-streaming site.

One day, I suddenly realized that there are many brothers outside this support group who struggle daily with impure thoughts and fall more regularly into porn and masturbation than those in the support group! Yet these folks have become so accustomed to their routine failures and perceived them as "common to man". They do not experience a godly sorrow that leads to confession and repentance like the brothers in the support group.

Since coming out, I have experienced definite victory over the battle against pornography and masturbation. However, sexual temptations remain real in my life. The support group has become the environment that God uses to keep me accountable and to practice the confession of sins to prevent bondage in this area of my life again. I therefore thank the brothers in the support group. It is they who have sharpened my sensitivity to sin. It is they who have taught me how to war against even the slightest hint of sensuality in my life.

Rick Toh
Lead Pastor
Yio Chu Kang Chapel

HEALING COMMUNITIES
– Reflection –

I have been discipling people in the area of sexuality for over five years. Four of those years were spent pioneering the ministry of sexual wholeness.[1] I met men and women working through issues of same-sex attraction and opposite-sex attraction. I walked with individuals struggling with homosexuality, and with their parents. Many had been suffering silently for years.

The *Whole Life Inventory*[2] reveals that 2 percent in our churches identify themselves as LGBTQ. Another 5 percent are unsure if they might be LGBTQ. Findings also indicate that many churches are not even teaching about sexuality.

In this section, five pastors address church culture toward people with same-sex attraction (SSA). I am fortunate to know these pastors. I will draw out insights and principles from their stories, and add personal reflections with practical pointers.

---

1   We cannot be spiritually healthy unless we are sexually healthy. Being healthy may indicate the absence of illness but may not indicate wholeness, which is having what is best and healthiest. The starting point of sexual wholeness is health. Health in its fullest and most complete sense is wholeness.

2   The *Whole Life Inventory* is a survey instrument for churches to assess the health of their congregations and understand the needs of their families in the Five Pillars—Faith, Identity, Relationships, Sexuality and Values.

Hon Chin Foang models the ground-up approach in shaping church culture towards people with SSA. He demonstrates the willingness to go the distance in mentoring them. For example, he has journeyed with one same-sex attracted member for 23 years. Pastor Hon embodies the relational approach that combines brotherly friendship with spiritual parenting.

Ian Toh exemplifies pastors who share their own stories of brokenness to provide safe places for those who are struggling with brokenness in various forms. In his approach, shepherds set the example and tone in vulnerability through narrating their own struggles with sexuality. Ian takes the lead with his no-holds-barred sharing that encourages the congregation to do likewise.

Andrew Cho speaks as a pastor with SSA who has himself journeyed with other same-sex attracted people. He highlights the need to understand the unique tensions faced by same-sex attracted believers. He also emphasizes the congregation as a community of healing.

Dev Menon emphasizes confession. He invites leaders to confess their sins to one another. Dev confesses to elders and pastors, then with staff and other leaders. Leaders, in turn are encouraged to confess their sins to the congregation. Of course this has to be done wisely but they needn't wait till they have victory over a sin to confess it.

Rick Toh's life is a classic example of authenticity. Leaders start authentic conversations with their spouses and, where appropriate, with their children. His son is an accountability partner. Rick started support groups for sexuality issues. Male leaders in his church share with other men in the congregation and female leaders share with other females.

Their stories highlight that leaders are spiritual environmental engineers. We get to set the culture of our churches towards those who struggle with sexual brokenness, to move from a climate of hostility to one of mercy—and we must.

We have done little to help our people who struggle sexually. The church has not done much to help followers of Jesus who have SSA deal with the reality of sexual frustration. Few acknowledge the high price paid by same-sex attracted individuals who become Christians. Suddenly these men and women are confronted by the reality of leaving close friends, long-term partners, and even supportive communities. Often they get no sympathy from adult Christians who think they should just repent and get on with life.

In contrast, the LGBTQ community offers a safe place and therefore is an attractive alternative to same-sex attracted people who feel that the church is inauthentic and judgemental. Strugglers and family members have been drawn to LGBTQ communities because they have not been able to share their pain with their own congregations. Their hurt is very deep and their shame is very real.

We pronounce same-sex practice unbiblical but no one offers solutions. It is irresponsible to preach against sin without offering alternatives. We can learn from the pro-life movement whose leaders offer help such as crisis counselling, emergency housing, and adoption services for pregnant women in addition to saying: "Don't kill your unborn child." When we call people to say "no" to homosexual behaviour to follow Jesus, what can our same-sex attracted members say "yes" to and what supportive structures will our churches offer so that their obedience to Jesus leads to a life of wholeness?

The majority of Christians who struggle with SSA and who remain chaste have the added struggle of remaining single. How can we call our singles, including our same-sex attracted members, to sexual abstinence if we don't create social environments that make such a life meaningful and viable? Constant encouragement and accountability from the congregation is important to continue on the road to wholeness. Accordingly, I suggest three positive pastoral initiatives.

First, create a healing community. Talk about what it means to create a community in which brokenness is accepted, where we are free to talk about messy pasts, learn the art of real listening, and embrace the fragile identities of those who have been rescued by Christ. This does not mean we share our deepest secrets with everyone, but we are able to be open with at least a few close friends, so that others can help bear our burdens and walk with us as we strive for godliness. People must feel safe before they can be free to share. The church needs to be a safe place where we can bring our humanness. Leaders need to model vulnerability to nurture this culture.

Take a relational approach. Create community structures where we can be a Christ-like family for each of us to carry one another's burdens and so fulfil the law of Christ. Prioritize intergenerational connectedness and authentic community. This is not just a programme. It requires a change of heart. Reject pseudo-intimacy. Teach people how to really love one another and how to offer grace to each other. Talk with people about opening their hearts to other people's struggles, teaching them how to listen and how to care with compassion. Help singles to experience different kinds of dates: five good friends going out and doing something together—some married and some single; or just singles learning how to gather a few friends to have fun together and to relate. We need to figure out how to help people experience new ways of relating.

Second, we need to disciple people in the area of sexuality. Right now, the church is not saying much to singles, who include same-sex attracted members, about sexuality. Instead we lift up a superficial view of what sexuality means to Christians—"Just don't do it", that is, no sex outside the covenant of marriage. Singles are not allowed to talk about their sexuality with reality and honesty. Where would our singles go to share about their pain and brokenness, as they struggle in their thought life or even in actual sexual expression?

Break the silence. Begin with clear teaching on the theology of sexuality, relationships, marriage and singlehood. God values singleness as much as marriage. Teach lifespan sexuality education. Talk about sexuality as openly and honestly as possible. Help mentors discuss sexuality with their spouses. Equip parents to disciple their own children in the area of sexuality. The good news is that young adults and youths are accepting of peers who struggle with sexual brokenness. Our young are ready to be discipled in sexuality and are willing to disciple others in turn.

Third, we need to learn about homosexuality. Many lack an understanding of SSA. Homophobia or the irrational fear of same-sex attracted people, often lead to people who are negative towards those who are same-sex attracted. This causes them grievous pain.

Get acquainted with the many layers of homosexuality. Teaching on this subject must be done within the wider context of a robust theology of sexuality. SSA is a romantic and/or sexual attraction to someone of the same sex. SSA is just one example of what it means to live in a broken world. No one chooses to feel attracted to someone of the same sex. But men and women do have a choice on how they will act on those feelings.

Get equipped to respond with both truth and grace so that people struggling with homosexuality will see and know that God loves all and wants to reclaim each one for His Kingdom. Then equip the church to journey with the struggling. Train the congregation in compassion. Differentiate between validation of the individual, which is ok, versus affirmation of behaviour, which is not. For instance, we continue to love and journey with cell members who struggle with overspending though we disagree with their behaviour.

Leaders often feel that we have to know everything. Actually, saying that you don't understand is how bridge-building starts. We need mentors and/or cell leaders who simply love the struggler and are there for him when he struggles and when he falls. People don't choose to be vulnerable to those who know the most, but to those who love us the most. Love each hurting man and woman. Be a father or mother figure to those who have never had one. Model the heart of the Father.

Historically, the church has had a reputation for being very strong on truth but severely lacking in grace when it comes to dealing with homosexual sin. Today the church finds itself under immense pressure from multiple directions to change her stance. It is easier and safer to just do nothing.

The stakes are high if we address the issue of homosexuality but the consequences are even higher if we don't. If the church does not respond adequately to the issues of SSA, strugglers will look to the surrounding culture for answers. A fallen world will conclude that the gospel has no relevance for those struggling with SSA. Families need to know that our congregations are safe places for broken people and that we are willing to extend God's unconditional love. The reason I support this book is because we need an honest pastoral conversation on SSA. Every day that we fail to do so, more same-sex attracted people will suffer the consequences of our inaction.

Ben KC Lee
Lead Pastor
RiverLife Church

ACKNOWLEDGEMENTS

This book has been a massive labour of love and would not have been possible without the trust, support, and commitment of many. We are immensely grateful to all who worked together tirelessly to produce this book within such a short timeframe.

For undertaking this project (the first book of this series), we are thankful to Micah Singapore.

The team from Graceworks provided invaluable support from conception to publishing.

We would like to express our heartfelt gratitude to every single one of our story contributors as well as our Foreword, Theological Overview, and Reflection writers (Rev Dr Robert Solomon, Dr Kwa Kiem Kiok, Raphael Zhang, Marianne Wong, and Pastor Ben KC Lee).

We are thankful to over 30 individuals and organizations who responded swiftly and gave generously to our crowdfunding effort.

We want to acknowledge Raphael Zhang for his insights, connections, and tireless effort through this project. We also thank Joanna Hor for volunteering to edit, as well as our proofreaders, Nicole Ong and Chris Tan, for poring over every page to smoothen any bumps.

We're especially grateful to Dr Wesley Hill who got us started on the journey of producing a book on this topic for the church in Singapore, and Dr Goh Wei Leong, who has been a steadfast supporter from start to end.

Finally, and most importantly, we want to give thanks to our Heavenly Father, without whom none of this would have been possible. He is the ultimate Good News for all bruised reeds.

HELP RESOURCES

At the Cross Gathering
A support group ministry for men who are struggling with sexual addiction and brokenness, At the Cross currently meets at Yio Chu Kang Chapel.
Contact: **atthecrossSG@gmail.com**
Contact Person: **Pastor Rick Toh**
Address: **242 Yio Chu Kang Road, Singapore 545671**

Bryan Shen
Bryan is a professional counsellor registered with the Singapore Association for Counselling. He gives educational talks to communities to remove misconceptions and prejudice, explain what SSA is, why it is not chosen, the harm of quack therapies, and what communities can do—in line with the Truth that exists in all faiths. He also gives deeper details in three-day trainings for counsellors, mental health professionals, religious leaders, and educators.
Website & Contact: **http://counsellorbryan.weebly.com**

Choices Ministry
This ministry in Church of Our Saviour was established in 1991 to help people recover their God-intended sexual identity. We offer support to individuals struggling with same-sex attraction, as well as for lesbian, gay, bisexual, transgender, and questioning (LGBTQ) individuals who are struggling with their sexual choices or lifestyle, includ-

ing family members of persons who identify themselves as LGBTQ.

Website: http://www.coos.org.sg/church-life/choices/
Contact: (+65) 8876 0143
Address: 130 Margaret Drive, Singapore 149300

Courage (Roman Catholic)

Persons living with same-sex attraction need to experience the freedom of interior chastity and in that freedom find support to live a fully Christian life in communion with God and others. Courage provides a spiritual support system which would assist men and women with same-sex attraction to live chaste lives in fellowship, truth and love.

Website: http://courage.org.sg
Contact: sdcourage.sg@gmail.com

Ellel Ministries Singapore

Ellel Ministries Singapore is focused on the restoration of broken lives through the healing and deliverance ministry of Jesus Christ.

Website: http://www.ellel.org/sg/
Contact: (+65) 6252 4234
Address: 39A Jalan Pemimpin, #05-01A, Halcyon Building, Singapore 577183

EnCourage (Roman Catholic)

EnCourage is a ministry for parents, family members and friends of loved ones with same-sex attraction. It offers a supportive, confidential environment to share feelings, experiences, information and guidance for maintaining healthy relationships with our loved ones with same-sex attraction.

Website: http://courage.org.sg/encourage/
Contact: http://courage.org.sg/contact-us/

Family Life Society

Family Life Society has a team of professional counsellors who provide support to those facing personal, marital and family issues. These issues may include pregnancy, sexuality or same-sex attraction.

Website: **http://familylife.sg** | Contact: **(+65) 6488 0278**
Address: **2 Highland Road, #LG-01, Singapore 549102**

Hope Oasis

Dare To Believe Prayer Ministry is a gentle, safe, biblical and practical method of confronting opposing spiritual forces that has assisted many individuals and families to be free of the physical, emotional and spiritual problems that have prevented them from knowing their true worth and identity as well as living in the full freedom of Christ. Utilizing the gifts of discernment, sight and intercession, this ministry targets a specific matter and prays for God's intervention and resolution for yourself or an organisation that you are a part of.

Website: **https://www.hopeoasis.org/**
Contact: **contact@hopeoasis.org or (+65) 6902 0087**
Address: **265 Joo Chiat Road, Singapore 427519**

Journey Asia in Singapore

Journey Singapore exists to help people find hope and live life through experiencing Jesus in their relationships, sexuality and identity. We carry out our mission by partnering with churches to offer safe places for spiritual care and experiential discipleship.

Website: **http://www.journeysingapore.org/**
Contact: **info@journeysingapore.org**

Luke 4:18 Ministry

Luke 4:18 Ministry offers professional counselling, inner healing, and support groups for people struggling with sexual brokenness addiction and issues.

Contact: **help@luke418ministry.sg**

Pursuing Liberty Under Christ

Pursuing Liberty Under Christ (PLUC) is a Christian non-profit organisation with a three-fold mission to relate to, advocate for, and educate on individuals struggling with same-sex attraction.

Website: http://www.pluc.org.my/
Contact: **+603-7887 3501 / +6012-508 3501 (Helpline)**
Address: **P.O. Box 8513, Pejabat Pos Kelana Jaya,
46791 Petaling Jaya, Selangor, Malaysia**

Restoring The Foundations Asia Pacific

Restoring The Foundations is a versatile discipleship and ministry tool that brings an individual through a time of ministry, empowering them to move forward in their calling and identity in Christ Jesus. Through dealing with the Four Ministry Areas, the Lord can effect and manifest His victory in their lives.

Website: **http://restoringthefoundations.asia/**
Contact: **office@restoringthefoundations.asia or
(+65) 6570 6007**
Address: **62 Bayshore Road, #29-01, Pearl Tower,
Bayshore Park, Singapore 469983**

Sexuality Counselling & Support Services

Focus on the Family Singapore offers professional counselling on issues of sexual brokenness for anyone who wishes to journey toward wholeness. It also offers faith-based support groups for people with same-sex attraction, and for parents with same-sex attracted children.

Website: https://www.wholelife.sg/sexualitycounselling

Contact: (+65) 6491 0700

Address: 9 Bishan Place, #08-03, Junction 8 Office Tower, Singapore 579837